# The Italian
# Road to Socialism

# The Italian Road to Socialism

**An Interview by Eric Hobsbawm with Giorgio Napolitano
of the Italian Communist Party**

*Translated by*
John Cammett & Victoria DeGrazia

Lawrence Hill & Company
*Westport, Connecticut*

The Journeyman Press
*London*

© 1977 in English translation by Lawrence Hill & Company, Publishers, Inc.
*First published in Great Britain, 1977, (ISBN 0 904526 24 0) by*
The Journeyman Press, 97 Ferme Park Road, Crouch End, London N8 9SA

Published in Italy by Gius. Laterza & Figli Spa
as *Intervista Sul PCI*

Library of Congress Catalog Card Number: LC: 77-83770

First U.S. Edition, October, 1977

ISBN: 0-88208-082-2 (cloth edition) 0-88208-089-X (paperback edition)

1    2    3    4    5    6    7    8    9    10

Lawrence Hill & Company, Publishers, Inc.
24 Burr Farms Road, Westport, Connecticut 06880

Jacket design by Robert McLeod

Manufactured in the United States of America

# The Italian
# Road to Socialism

## Publisher's Note

*The Italian Road to Socialism* is a collection of interviews by the internationally respected British historian Eric J. Hobsbawm with Giorgio Napolitano, the economic spokesman of the Italian Communist Party. The first interview took place in Rome on October 1 & 2, 1975. Hobsbawm and Napolitano resumed their discussions on March 19, 1977, in London, and this material constitutes the second interview, bringing the earlier conversations up to date.

The book focuses on what may be the most significant political development in Western Europe since World War II—the rise of Euro-Communism. Among the questions raised are:

- How does the new political reality affect U.S. relations with Italy?
- What has been the significance of the 1976 Italian elections?
- What is "the historic compromise"?
- Is the PCI loyal first to Moscow or to Italy and NATO?
- What economic programs does the PCI propose, and how can the Party work within the capitalist system?
- How much real power has the Italian Communist Party today?

# The Italian
# Road to Socialism

# I

**ERIC J. HOBSBAWM:** *Before we start, let me ask you one thing: will you reply to my questions as a member of the Secretariat of the Communist Party? Could you clarify this?*

**GIORGIO NAPOLITANO:** I shall not always claim to speak for the Party. Naturally, I'll try to take account of everything which we have developed collectively, but I shall try above all to respond to your questions on the basis of the *experience* of my generation in the Party.

**H.** *All right. Let us begin with your personal experience, since that seems to be a very useful point of departure. How did you come to the Communist Party—through what series of thoughts and developments?*

**N.** I came to the Communist Party during 1944 and 1945. I had already "discovered" the Communists at the time of the final crisis of fascism, when I was entering the University, but at that time my orientation was primarily antifascist. From 1944 to 1945, the bases were laid for the development of the Communist

Party as a mass party. In the North, that came about in the fire of the Resistance movement, the war for liberation. In Southern Italy—and this is worth emphasizing—this process occurred in a profoundly different context. In both the North and the South, young people from the ranks of petty bourgeoisie or the middle-class intelligentsia also joined the Communist Party. In South Italy this choice had a strong political and moral basis strictly connected to the situation existing in that part of Italy after the fall of fascism and the liberation by the allied armies.

To those of us who joined the Communist Party in Naples or other regions of the South, the Party meant first of all the most uncompromising force of antifascist struggle, which at that time was engaged in the forefront of the Resistance in the partisan movement. Even in the South, where the Party participated in the government, it was fighting to promote a united contribution to the war for liberating that part of North Italy still occupied by the Nazis. This image of the Italian Communist Party was reinforced by its being part of a great world movement, at the head of which stood the Soviet Union. For all of us, the Soviet Union's heroic and victorious contribution to the offensive against the Nazi forces was a great and extraordinary attraction.

But to return to the most important reasons for our joining the PCI, I believe we should emphasize the role of the Communist Party in the struggle to resolve the grave problems inherited from fascism, especially in the South.

**H.** *How did the PCI react to these problems?*

**N.** One really must make an effort to recall the situation in Naples and the South when Togliatti returned to Italy in 1944. Some years later, Togliatti himself wrote a very fine testimony on how Naples struck him then. The city was a repository for all the elements of disintegration and Southern backwardness, and the ruins and devastation caused by the war were particularly dreadful.

How could this situation be remedied in view of the political backwardness of the South? In the North many advanced positions had been won by the labor movement through the Resistance; in the South, both in the cities—even in large cities like Naples—and in the countryside, the influence of reactionary forces was still dominant. The Communist Party seemed to so many of us that force which could best assure a radical change and achieve at the same time the widest possible unity for the liberation and reconstruction of the country. In the South, it seemed best equipped to work for reform, political and social redemption and the promotion of consciousness raising in the great popular masses. With this prospect and these objectives in mind, it had taken on governmental responsibilities immediately after Togliatti's return to Italy—thanks to the new direction he gave to Italian politics.

We also felt a personal need fully to commit ourselves to this work of reconstruction and renewal, work which was extremely difficult under the conditions existing in Naples and the South. There were many young people like me, who came from the ranks of the petty bourgeoisie or the middle-class intelligentsia, who felt at that moment that they had to make a total commitment, putting aside their individual projects and those of a cultural or professional character: a total commitment within the party of the working class. This then was the political and moral basis for our move toward the PCI. Our ideological training came later.

**H.** *How did the convergence of the young Southerners with the "Turinese" tradition of the Italian labor and Communist movement come about?*

**N.** A very important bridge, if you wish to call it that, was constituted by some Party leaders who were already proven leaders of the first rank, who had themselves been, in their time, young Southern intellectuals. Through the experience of the antifascist struggle and of prison, banishment and emigration, these young men had become organically fused with the group of leaders of working-class origin and "Turinese" tradition. I am speaking of men like Giorgio Amendola and Emilio Sereni. They were the ones who took charge of the Party activity in South Italy immediately after the liberation of the North. There is no doubt that they represented a particularly significant tie between the new generations of Southern Communists and the national leadership of the Party, which was still largely rooted, as you said, in the Turinese experience where they were trained under Gramsci.

It must be said that the Party leadership as a whole—partly working in the North during the war of liberation and partly already present in the South—under the leadership of Togliatti was a great source of reassurance and attraction for us, almost to the point of idolatry. It stood for what had been historically the heroic commitment of the Communists in the struggle against fascism, not only in Italy but also in Europe. At the same time, it represented the deep bond of the Italian Communist Party with the whole world Communist movement.

**H.** *You said that your ideological training came afterward. This seems to me to be completely normal. In general, political commitment precedes ideological and theoretical development.*

**N.** On the other hand, there was intense theoretical debate among young intellectuals in the thirties, even before they joined the Party clandestinely. I'm thinking especially of the Roman group, men like Lucio Lombardo Radice, Aldo Natoli, Paolo Bufalini, and then Mario Alicata, Pietro Ingrao, to recall only a few. The effort to develop ideological coherence was an important component of the very act of enrolling in the Party. Instead, we joined during a situation which was both very dramatic and very exciting; hence, we joined more impulsively.

**H.** *What were the stages of your theoretical and idological development after you joined the Party?*

**N.** I must say that our main commitment consisted in going "to the school of the working class." In these days the expression might seem rhetorical, but then in a city like Naples the core of the Party really was its worker cadres. For us, it was indeed a rather severe school. Our main efforts were aimed at learning to discipline our work and learning the problems of the working class and of the labor movement so that we could become effective political cadres. I think I may say that this demanding effort was carried out modestly and seriously by a great many of us.

With regard to our training in ideas and culture, the discussion is far from simple. I refer to what was for many years the usual position of the Party in this respect. Basically, we were asked to work in two distinct areas. One was to forge links with traditional culture and especially with traditional Southern culture, both in its more progressive positions—to which we as Marxists and Communists wished to appeal—and in its more complex and intellectual aspects, toward which we needed to develop a rigorous critical attitude. On the second level—the history of Italy, the history of the South, the Italian cultural tradition—we got much help and inspiration with the publication of Gramsci's *Letters* and *Prison Notebooks*.

The other direction to which we were committed, one clearly distinct and separate, was the scholastic study of the fundamental theoretical positions of Marxism-Leninism, even, and particularly, in its most rigid and simplified versions: famous texts such as Stalin's *Principles of Leninism* and the *History of the Communist Party (Bolshevik) of the Soviet Union*.

Thus, two very different activities coexisted in the cultural work of the Party and, therefore, in the ideological and cultural education of each of us. Still, it must be said that we younger Party militants had no sense of the contradictions between the two elements of our cultural education. Actually, the contradiction came to light much later with the attack on the dogmatic distortions of Marxism and the restrictive postures of cultural politics typical of the Stalinist period.

**H.** *So far, we have emphasized the period of the struggle for liberation, because it is the logical point of departure for an analysis of the PCI. Yet I think that before that period the Party had a history of discontinuity, whereas after the Liberation its development was substantially continuous. Before tracing the development of the PCI from 1944 to 1945, it would seem important to establish the historical heritage, the specific situations and experiences, which had shaped the Party that you and others of your generation entered between 1943 and 1945.*

**N.** I agree that it's important to reflect on the historical process through which the PCI and its politics became what they were at the time. It is correct to emphasize one particular aspect—and I want to do so in reference to an essential characteristic of the PCI—which appeared immediately after the fall of fascism. The PCI emerged as a major democratic force, a champion of the authentic values of freedom and democracy. Even if other political forces and major currents of opinion questioned the democratic character of the Communist Party, or the genuine quality of its democratic commitment, we knew that it had in fact demostrated its belief and its ability to contribute in the most effective way to the struggle for freedom and democracy.

Still, at that time, we were not entirely aware of the enormous difficulties that had been involved in making the Communist Party the most consistent defender of the struggle for freedom and democracy.

**H.** *One moment, please. Freedom and democracy are fine, but weren't you also thinking of socialism and the socialist revolution?*

**N.** None of the young people like me who joined the Communist Party in those years doubted that the final objective had to be socialism, a transformation of society in the socialist sense. But in '44–'45 the immediate objectives seemed those of the liberation of the North, which was still occupied by the Nazis, and thereafter the founding of a new democractic state. We wanted a democratic regime open to further developments and transformations in a socialist sense—what Togliatti called a regime of progressive democracy. I repeat, however, that we did not know at that time and we did not learn until much later how difficult it was to win those immediate goals involved with progressive democracy. Perhaps this is the point which interests you.

**H.** *Yes, that was precisely the point of my question.*

**N.** I think that the peculiar historical circumstance of being the first of the Communist parties forced to confront fascism, to experience the defeat of the labor movement at fascist hands and to engage in the long and difficult search for an effective form of struggle against fascism was absolutely decisive for the Italian Communist Party and its future. For a number of years, these vicissitudes were experienced by the Italian Communist Party alone, though of course the problem was the subject of discussion in the international Communist movement. The Italian Communist Party was first obliged to undergo that terrible experience, and it was ever after marked by it. Even today, we cannot understand what makes the PCI different without turning to its history: it had to deal with fascism.

Only in the thirties did the question of fascism and the struggle against it become a general problem in all Europe. Within the Communist International, as we know, there were many complex discussions during the twenties and thirties. There was a long history of conflicting positions before arriving at the famous Seventh Congress of the International in 1935. In the Italian Party, however, I would say that reflection on the defeat of the labor movement by fascism had already become very important in the years between 1923 and 1926.

**H.** *But perhaps we are dealing here with a double defeat and not just the one by fascism. Earlier the revolutionary perspective had failed, at the time of the occupation of the factories. In the postwar period, the Italian political situation had been among the most dramatic in Western Europe, and the Italian labor movement was the particular victim of its unhappy outcome.*

**N.** The facts demonstrated the correctness of Gramsci's prediction of 1920, according to which either the revolutionary movement of the working class would find an opening or there would be a "tremendous reaction" on the part of the propertied classes. The ebbing of the revolutionary movement and the defeat by fascism are two events intimately bound to one another. In the years from 1923 to 1926, when Gramsci reflected on the experience of the preceding years, he investigated both the reasons for the waning of the revolutionary movement (returning painfully to what happened in 1919 and 1920) as well as the reasons for the victory of fascism. In those years he was already beginning to develop a line for overcoming the errors of sectarianism and schematism which had favored the victory of fascism. Reflection and research on those themes continued for many years. They were developed both by Gramsci's work in prison and by the Party as it continued to work outside of Italy and within Italy. Gradually the road was mapped out to avoid new defeats in the future and, above all, to defeat fascism by achieving the vastest possible front for the struggle against it.

**H.** *And how were you able to find this road?*

**N.** After extremely conflicting and dramatic discussions in the International, it was found at the Seventh Congress by selecting the line of the broadest unity of antifascist forces. There the labor and Communist movements took a clear position in espousing fully the need to defend all the bourgeois democratic freedoms. Finally, in the light of the experience of the Spanish Republic, the Communists—Togliatti in particular—elaborated the prospect of a "democracy of a new type."

Why was it so important to develop this prospect? Because it made possible a resolution of the dilemma of whether the objective of the struggle against fascism was to restore bourgeois democracy as the social democratic forces wished (this is what the Communist Parties charged them with) or if the objective of the struggle against fascism was to establish the dictatorship of the proletariat, as the Communists had maintained at the time when the politics of the International were most restrictive. This false dilemma, so paralyzing to efforts to unify the antifascist forces, and especially the Communist, socialist and social-democratic forces, was resolved—for the Italian Communist Party, for Togliatti—by the development of this new perspective: the objective of the struggle against fascism is neither to establish the dictatorship of the proletariat nor to restore bourgeois democracy purely and simply. It is to create a democratic regime of a new type, which overcomes the limits and the fundamental defects of prefascist democracy and which is open to the possibility of successive developments and profound transformations in a socialist sense.

**H.** *Here you've touched upon an interesting point. The theory of a democracy of a new type, as you call it, was not solely and strictly an Italian perspective. The English Communist Party discussed this problem too, at the Seventh Congress. But certainly the experience of the Italians—their analysis of fascism, their development of the problems of what Gramsci called a war of position rather than a war of movement—all this made the thought and struggle of the Italian Communist Party more rele-*

*vant for the development of this perspective than the contributions which came from other countries.*

*I wonder if there has not been something else in the objective situation of Italy which has contributed toward making the role of the Italian Communist Party so central. After all, Italy occupies a singular place in bourgeois capitalist development in Europe. Even in the period between the two wars, I think that Italy, if I may put it this way, belonged neither to the third world nor to the first world.*

**N.**  I think that the historical conditions of Italy's backwardness as a capitalist country certainly contributed toward pushing the Italian Communist Party to emphasize questions concerning the democratic revolution. Let us simply recall the work done, even before the Party was outlawed, on the fundamental themes of the Southern question and the peasant question. However, we did increasingly and consciously try to take as our point of departure the historical fact of the persistence of precapitalist residues in an important part of the country and thence to develop a perspective in which the struggle for democracy and the struggle for socialism would be fused. Even at the beginning of the fifties —with regard to the development of the united popular movement for the rebirth of the South—some members of our party held that the objective of the struggle in Southern Italy was purely and simply the completion of the bourgeois democratic revolution. That point of view was challenged, correctly I think, by precisely those comrades who were most involved in Party work in the South and in the battle for reform in the South. On the other hand, right after the Resistance and even at the height of the Resistance, some of us had emphasized that a democratic revolution was under way in Italy and was to be encouraged but not confined within the limits of a pure bourgeois democratic revolution. Objective and subjective conditions were present so that this change and renewal of a democratic character might possibly develop on a new level in the direction of socialism.

**H.** *But in that period, a clear distinction was made regarding the problem of democracy: The idea was surely to restore and develop democracy without falling back into the transformism of bourgeois liberal democracy.*

**N.** It was not only a question of this. I should like to recall another characteristic element in the experience of the PCI, which helps to explain the particularly relevant contributions which it made to the development of a new prospect for the whole Communist movement in Europe. I am thinking especially of its development of the analysis of fascism, of its class nature and basic characteristics. From this, it developed a position which became essential for advancing the debate on democracy: that is, the need to eradicate the roots of fascism and especially its economic and social roots. When we spoke of a democracy of a new type, which was not merely a restoration of prefascist democracy, we were not referring solely to the transformistic and parliamentary degenerations of the prefascist democratic regime, but rather to the need to give an advanced economic and social content to democracy. Above all, we intended to build an economic regime which eradicated the roots of fascism—and, therefore, the possibility for its rebirth—through structural reforms, through far-reaching reforms in the economic and social structures. In comparison with prefascist democracy, this was and is an essential and distinctive element of the democracy of a new type which we wished to build.

**H.** *This brings us to problems regarding the strategy of the Communist Party after the war. You assert that it was necessary to uproot and destroy the social basis of fascism through struc-*

*tural reforms in order to prevent a return to the old bourgeois democracy, to the kind of democracy which led to the birth of fascism. Within this framework, what were the main objectives of the Communist Party?*

**N.** Beginning in '44–'45, the PCI laid out a series of reforms. The first was an agrarian reform which struck at large landed property and especially at absentee owners of large estates. Another project was what was then defined as "industrial reform," which would have limited the power of the large monopolistic groups by increasing the role of the democratic state in economic planning. At that time, we also tried to develop new forms of mass participation and to move toward a more united and diversified democratic organization of the working and popular masses. Our main concerns were both to prevent the reappearance of a political and social climate which would allow reactionary forces to reorganize and take the initiative and to erode the power positions of the old ruling classes in order to prevent the reconstruction of their bases for a reactionary and fascist counteroffensive.

**H.** *How did you resolve the problems of the democratic organization of the masses?*

**N.** Above all, by breaking with the fascist heritage and inspiring the organized labor movement toward priniciples of freedom and real participation. Recently, the Party archives have published documents related to negotiations undertaken in the early months of 1944—in Rome, which was still occupied by the Nazis—among Communists, socialists and Catholics for the creation of a united trade union confederation. Giuseppe Di Vittorio, who led the negotiations for our party, was confronted with opposition from socialists and also from Catholics who favored retaining within the new democracy the single, obligatory trade union legally created by fascism. Their interests lay in the growth in membership and power which would come through compulsory membership and the automatic payment of dues. Anyone reading those documents today will be impressed by the authority, not to say vehemence, with which Di Vittorio attacked that position. He praised and emphasized the workers' "need for freedom" after twenty years of odious restrictions and maintained that a legally obligatory trade union would be a bureaucratic organism with "a lot of money, and many offices and employees," but "detested by the working class." What was needed was a fully democratic trade union which "left the main initiative and authority to the masses." With the Pact of Rome of June, 1944, his line was accepted and became the basis for the creation of a united trade union confederation in free Italy.

It follows, of course, that this line included enormous difficulties. For many years, it was extremely difficult freely to create and consolidate a mass trade union, especially in certain regions of the South. But the idea of an organization based on the democratic initiative of the masses was one of the keys, and it still is, for preventing the resurgence of fascism, and for building a democracy of a new type. If we still want to use a term of thirty years ago, this would be a progressive democracy: a democracy exceeding the limits of traditional bourgeois democracy. Certainly, it would not yet be a socialist democracy, because the bases of the state and society would not yet have been changed in a socialist sense.

**H.** *Therefore, at that time you were trying to build the foundation for a move toward socialism. But how did you conceive of the transition to socialism? Did you see it as a long process?*

**N.** Undoubtedly as a long-term process. A rapid transition to socialism was absolutely not in our perspective. This seemed clear even to those of us who joined the party while the dramatic war of liberation was raging in the North.

**H.**   *That raises two questions. One criticism which has been made from that time on hinges on the thesis that there was the possibility of moving with greater speed toward socialism. Why, in other words, did the Communist Party not try to take power during 1944 and 1945?*

**N.**   It is entirely understandable that discussions of this kind were raised even in our own ranks at the time of the Resistance and immediately after in the regions which had gone through the Resistance and had won important gains for the labor movement. But even there the political line of the Party as developed by Togliatti and the leading group prevailed completely. I refer to his line of unity for the reconstruction of the country, for the launching of structural reforms and for the foundation of a new democratic state.

It is true that in recent years there have also been discussions on the possibilities offered by the Italian situation immediately after the Liberation. One of the political criticisms "from the left" with regard to us had indeed been the allegation that we failed to exploit the "historical opportunity" and the revolutionary possibilities offered by the war of liberation and its victorious outcome. It seems to me that these assessments have found slight support and have not been persuasive.

Even in the historiographical field, more balanced judgments have prevailed. This corresponds with the experience of those who lived through that period and especially with those who lived not in the North but in the South. Such persons were aware of the concrete reality of two Italys and of the existence of an extremely contradictory reality in the country as a whole. They were conscious at that time of the perils of a division, of an historical fissure between North and South, and they were guided by a realistic consideration of the relations of force existing on the level of class and politics in the Italy of that time. Moreover, there was the international situation to be considered, the special condition of Italy, which was still occupied by the allied armies and already firmly included within a certain political and military area.

**H.**  *I am sure that the Italian situation in '44–'45 did not allow a revolutionary solution, even if many wanted it. On the other hand, a second criticism in this regard is possible, a criticism perhaps founded on more realistic grounds. You say that it was then necessary to destroy the bases of fascism. I wonder, however, if those bases were, in fact, destroyed. Was the resurgence of a bourgeois democracy of the old type really prevented?*

**N.**  A process of renewal aimed at the destruction of the roots of fascism and the construction of a democracy of a new type was launched and did achieve some results in the period between 1944 and 1947. But this democratic or antifascist revolution, as we call it, was brusquely interrupted with the appearance of the Cold War internationally and with the rupture of the unity of antifascist forces on the internal level, when the socialists and Communists were excluded from the government in the Spring of 1947. Thereafter, a throughgoing regression in the Italian political situation prevented us from attaining more substantial results. Although our aim was neither the conquest of power by the working class nor a rapid transition to socialism, it was nonetheless an aim of profound transformation.

The fact is, however, that some of the achievements of '44–'47 continued in effect through the next period. They served as strongholds for resisting the antidemocratic and anticommunist offensive and for holding open the possibilities of a relaunching of the antifascist revolution.

**H.** *During the war of liberation, there surely was a broad hegemony of the labor and antifascist movement. Yet one suspects that at the end of the war excessive faith in this hegemony led to the neglect of the need to destroy effectively the social and institutional basis of fascism. Did not the combination of Christian Democracy and a substantially unchanged bureaucratic apparatus permit the "capitalist restoration"?*

**N.** I don't want to be misunderstood. What I said does not mean we did not commit errors between '44 and '47. On several occasions in the course of the last ten years and more, we ourselves have sought to single out some of the errors committed in the period following the Liberation: errors committed on the level of action for reforms and a new political economy; errors or insufficiencies on the level of action toward renovating the State. You have particularly referred to this last problem. There is no doubt that not only did we not succeed in effecting specific modifications in the institutional sector, but we also probably undervalued the need for those modifications. It is, therefore, true that in a number of respects we can still see a substantial continuity between the structures of the fascist and prefascist state and the structures of the postfascist state. The conservative administration of Christian Democracy—and the subsequent construction of the power system of a Christian Democracy—was grafted onto this continuity.

I have no doubt that we need more careful thought and self-critical research on this point. We need especially to achieve greater lucidity and concrete knowledge for our future dealings with the questions which are still open concerning the reform and renovation of the state.

**H.** *What would you say has remained from the period of the Resistance and the first years after the Liberation that is positive and permanent for Italy, for the labor movement and for the Communist Party?*

**N.** Above all, there remains a common political fabric, an inspiration and bond. Certainly this only operated in a very limited way during the period of the headon conflict between the various forces of the antifascist alignment, but in the sixties it again began to work effectively. The patrimony of antifascist unity remained as a political fact capable of revival, and of revival with the new and decisive support of the younger generations. In the second place, there remained the whole initial effort to build an organized democratic movement. In those years, a qualitative change came about in Italian society with the promotion to participation in political and social life of masses who historically had remained on the fringe, especially the peasant masses and lower classes of the South.

**H.** *The awakening of the South . . .*

**N.** Yes, the awakening of the South which had already begun in those years. Much work was done there in the years after '47–'48, but the point of departure and the first events—such as the movement to occupy uncultivated lands—took place in the South immediately after the Liberation. For their part, the Communists acted both from below and from above to promote this awakening. I repeat, also from above: One example was the political action carried out in the government by a Communist Minister of Agriculture, Fausto Gullo, who issued decrees for the concession of uncultivated or poorly cultivated lands to the peasants.

At the same time in the North (and also in the great industrial centers of the South, like Naples), the working class gained a leading role in the reconstruction and productive development of the country. This gain became permanent and characteristic of the Italian situation.

Finally, we have the Constitution. The work of the Constituent Assembly ended after the Communists had been ousted from the government, but still the task was successfully completed.

The Constitution establishes a frame of reference; it affords points of strength to the labor and democratic movements, the enormous value of which was only to be seen in later years. Today, the Constitution is still an important basis for the further development of the battle for the removal of society. The constitutional Charter sanctions extremely advanced democratic principles, even with regard to the democratic organization of the state—principles to which we can validly refer in the battle for reform which is still to be won.

**H.** *We might add two or three other observations. One is the fact of the historical continuity of the Communist Party as a mass movement and a major and never negligible factor in national life. Secondly, non-Italians are impressed by the dramatic emergence and subsequent persistence of cultural hegemony of anti-fascist, democratic and progressive elements in Italian national life (as distinct from West Germany where a whole generation had to pass while the older conservative traditions were broken. In Italy, after the end of the war, it almost seemed that intellectuals of the right no longer existed.*

*Thirdly, we foreigners are struck by the fact that the Italian people in some ways have liquidated the fascist heritage through mass antifascist struggles. Therefore, the great majority of the people does not bear the weight of having been fascist. All this forms a permanent base which excludes at least some negative political possibilities from the future of Italy.*

**N.** The gains and results to which you refer were in part achieved in '44–'47; in part, they were substantially confirmed and consolidated in later years, during which there might well have been a serious retreat. If that did not happen, if after the defeat of 1948 the PCI continually increased its influence with each election, then it is due to our political action during the years of the Cold War. During this time we even succeeded in consolidating the hegemony of antifascism and the labor movement among the intellectuals.

I consider the experience of the years of the Cold War as no less important than that of the years immediately after the Liberation and perhaps even that of the Resistance. A no less important experience.

**H.** *Then let us talk about the period after 1947, the Cold War.*

**N.** I'll discuss this period in connection with the problem of the continuity of development of the Communist Party. The continuity which you emphasized of the politico-electoral growth of the Communist Party can be explained only if we take account of the continuity of its politics and the continual improvement of some of its characteristic and fundamental preferences. First among these is its commitment to the defense and development of democracy. Even today, and even outside of Italy when some people comment on the views of the Communist Party in defense of democracy or for an advance to socialism within democracy, they interpret such statements, whether they are for or against, as though they were dealing with a simple declaration of faith.

Actually, however, our views in this area are something quite different. They are the result of an experience, the point of arrival of a long and laborious process. They are the very substance of the work undertaken for decades by the Party. In those years of the Cold War, in those years when Christian Democracy had the absolute majority in parliament and, in practice, the political monopoly, we continued to develop the implications of our choice of democracy. We identified ourselves with a whole series of values of freedom and, therefore, became its champions. We had to defend freedom's values against a political force which gravely restricted democratic rights and was in open violation of the democratic principles sanctioned in the republican Constitution.

It was then that we Communists became, in the eyes of great masses of Italian citizens, the most consistent defenders—together with the socialists, who shared with us the responsibilities of the opposition—first of all of the freedom of the working class (its freedom to organize and to struggle), of union rights, but also more generally of political freedom (which was also subjected to a strong obscurantist offensive), of cultural freedom and also of the prerogatives of the parliament. We responded to an attack aimed at mortally wounding our party by defending not only ourselves and our rights but also the rights of everyone and the democratic regime itself. In those years, some even played with the idea of outlawing the Communist Party, but we never limited ourselves to the mere defense of our party. This was an essential point.

**H.** *Are there other activities of that period to which you attribute special importance?*

**N.** Special importance can be attributed to the fact that our opposition was not purely negative or propagandistic. We lived through years of truly frontal collision. The dominant forces and the governments led by the Christian democracy tried to shatter the popular movement with all kinds of intimidation and discrimination. Our party and the left alignment responded with radical opposition. But at the same time, we always made an effort to indicate a possible solution for the country's problems—that is, not merely limit ourselves to denunciation, criticism and struggle in our confrontations with the government but also to outline an alternative, different and possible political program for the economic, social, civil and cultural progress of the nation. This too was very important. In those years, we did not lose the characteristics of a party of government, of a potential force for governing. We did not obscure the ruling function which the working class had claimed and in some measure exercised earlier, in the years immediately following the Liberation.

Let me recall the experience and the example of the "Plan for Labor" proposed in 1949 and 1950 by the General Confederation of Italian Labor (CGIL). That was an example of great initiative on the part of the labor movement during a period when it was on the defensive and in considerable difficulty. I want to recall the example of the CGIL's "Plan for Labor" because if we are interested not just in developments in the Communist Party but also in the Italian labor movement as a whole we must take account of this peculiar characteristic of our trade union movement: It has not limited itself to the pure defense of immediate interests, to simply demanding economic improvements for employed workers. Instead, it has also posed the problem of meeting the general interests of the popular masses and of the country as a whole by taking a stand on the larger questions of political and social economy.

**H.** *Indeed, I think it is very important that the Communist Party never let itself become isolated by its adversaries but continued to play a political role through participation in national politics. On the other hand, the years from 1947 to 1954 were years of defensive struggle during which the Communist Party did lose certain positions and possibilities. Do you think that was a consequence of the climate of the Cold War?*

**N.** The climate of those years was really very harsh. In the period of American atomic monopoly and the Korean War, I recall very well how the danger of a Third World War seemed real and near at hand, if not practically inevitable. In that same period, NATO was created with Italy in it. This too increased our concern, and our opposition was clear and radical. They were years in which a life-and-death struggle seemed at hand for the whole world Communist and labor movements. The policy then was explicitly aimed at pushing back the frontiers of the socialist world as they had been drawn up following World War II. The consequence of that climate was the acceptance by our party of solidarity and total identification with the socialist world.

But today we must say that that choice drove us to some mistaken attitudes, attitudes which now seem unacceptable to us. Because of this, we ended up by justifying the interventions of the Communist Party of the Soviet Union and other Communist Parties with state power in cultural and artistic life. Such interventions ended in the radical condemnation of certain tendencies, thus attributing to the Party a drastic, decision-making authority in matters relative to literary, artistic, cultural and even scientific research. In effect, our assumption of these justificatory attitudes reflected the fact that we ourselves had not yet succeeded in correctly resolving some problems. We hadn't yet elaborated our vision of the relations between politics and culture, between the party of the working class and culture.

More generally, we must say that our choice of total solidarity with the socialist world resulted in casting a shadow on our prospects for the advance of socialism in Italy. It gave rise to the suspicion that those prospects were substantially similar to the type of socialist society and administration of power existing in the Soviet Union and the popular democracies. For a long time, this suspicion was costly; it slowed and limited the development of our influence and our policy of alliances.

**H.** *I am also interested in another aspect of events in the PCI and the labor movement in the fifties: losses within the working class in the North and the weakening of the peasant movement in the South after the great struggles of 1949–50. How do you explain these facts?*

**N.** A number of diverse factors explain them, but here I wish to present only one: the changes in certain objective conditions (the maturing of a new process of development in Italian society) and our delay in taking account of them and adequately changing our political action. This brought about our growing difficulties in the large factories and also the snags we encountered in the Southern battle. It is a singular fact, in this respect, that we ourselves had contributed greatly to creating the "new" situation in the Southern countryside, which we then were slow to understand. Objectively, at a certain point the phase of the struggle for the conquest of uncultivated land ended and new problems opened up with the beginning of the reforms promulgated by the central governments. This created a new basis of struggle for the peasant masses whose composition and social situation were changing. We had trouble in adapting to these problems, which became in the course of later years problems in the orientation of agricultural production, problems of the market, problems of relations with individual industries and also with large monopolistic industry. More generally, we were slow to realize that the great phase of expansion of the Italian and the world economy was beginning.

**H.** *In fact the Italian economy was part of that world economy which in the fifties had begun the greatest expansion in the history of capitalism. Why do you think the PCI—though it was by no means alone in this—failed to recognize that turning point in capitalist history? After all, it was from the beginning more than a simple stabilization of capitalism?*

**N.** We Communists were conditioned by a political situation which led us to denounce the conservative and regressive aspects of the politics of the ruling classes as well as all the negative aspects of the economic and social situation. I believe that this played a role in preventing us from seeing more quickly the new developments which were maturing.

The problem is complex and is related to schematic positions, which were still present in our ranks, regarding the evaluation of capitalism and its possibilities of development in the monopolistic phase. The idea circulated, and in some measure influenced us, that stagnation in the development of productive forces and of production was an essential trait of capitalism in the present historical phase. We particularly underrated the disposable reserves of Italian capitalism as well as the international and internal conditions which could make for a period of intense, tumultuous economic development in Italy. Therefore, in the first half of the fifties, the incubational phase of the "economic miracle" escaped our attention.

**H.** *Now, the "great boom" is over. Retrospectively, however, what do you see as the main characteristics of the capitalist expansion in Italy during the fifties and sixties?*

**N.** We have had many discussions of the meaning of the expansion of the Italian economy which, as you know, became exceptionally intense between 1958 and 1963. Actually we discussed it when it still gave no signs of flagging and seemed destined to liquidate historical problems like that of the South not a few people thought it would.

In 1962, we held a meeting at the Instituto Gramsci on the tendencies of Italian capitalism. The evaluation which we made there has been amply confirmed both by later and recent experiences and by the work of the most serious scholars. We said that the ongoing expansion would undoubtedly lead to a profound change in the economic and social structure of the country, but that it was at the same time characterized by contradictions and grave disequilibria, the effects of which would eventually lead to a crisis for that kind of development. Thus, capitalism had counted upon the large supplies of labor-power in the countryside and the South, partly with the idea of breaking the labor market and keeping wages low, but this calculation proved to be mistaken. The consequent disregard of agriculture and the South would have become more and more a contradiction and a fatal weight for the further development of the Italian economy.

Moreover, the expansion of the fifties and sixties (remember that 1964 began a much more unstable decade, characterized by periods of recession and advance) was a function of foreign demand and exports, since Italy was clearly anchored to a subordinate position within the framework of the international division of labor. Italy did participate in that fabulous world expansion of capitalism to which you referred, but it participated from a position which then exposed it, more than other countries, to the consequences of the later recession and crisis of the capitalist economies.

**H.** *So it was possible to identify, as early as the beginning of the sixties, the particular and specific weaknesses of the Italian expansion?*

**N.** I would certainly say yes.

**H.** *The great capitalist boom was in certain ways a period of profound uncertainty about the prospects of the working class movement; but in fact the Party's strategic program was formulated and developed precisely in these years both in terms of domestic politics and the international arena—the program of the Italian road to socialism. How did this come about?*

**N.** For the entire 1950s and 1960s I would say there was, on the one hand, an intertwining of reasons for and times of uncertainty and difficulty, and on the other of new, extremely important developments in our policies. The turning point of 1956 was decisive. In the course of that crucial year, we made an important effort to work out a coherent outlook on the important questions underlining the advance toward socialism. This effort was essentially a response to the serious questions posed by the Twentieth Congress of the Communist Party of the Soviet Union (and later by the tragic events in Hungary). It meant acquiring and developing all the positive stimuli, all the new theoretical and political orientations which came out of the Twentieth Congress. We then tried to solve problems whose existence we had not even admitted during the Cold War, in the period preceding the CPSU Twentieth Congress especially up to 1953 and 1954.

In this context, we also, more specifically, carried out a critical evaluation of our political positions of the preceding years. We tried to free ourselves from the schematic concepts which had kept us from fully understanding the new elements which had emerged in the Italian socio-economic and political situations. At the same time, we rejected the opportunist interpretations of these new elements, those tendencies to overestimate "neocapitalist" development and to yield ground ideologically and politically; we raised the prospect of socialism in terms that were better adapted to Italian realities and more persuasive. This is not to deny, naturally, that in the years that followed—particularly in the 1960s—other serious reasons for and periods of uncertainty and confusion arose inside the Italian workers' movement in relation to changes both in the economic situation and of the political situation.

**H.** *Let's now turn to 1956. The Twentieth Congress was received in different ways by the different Communist Parties. The PCI drew from it much more far-reaching conclusions and position than did the others. Can this fact be explained by saying that, freed from the constraints of Stalinism, the Party took the occasion of the Twentieth Congress to develop its own line?*

**N.** The Italian Party had suffered greatly from the fact that in 1947, on an international level, the search for new roads to socialism had been abruptly cut off by the Communist movement, even though this search had been undertaken right after the end of the Second World War and not only in Italy. The Italian Party had suffered particularly, because it had advanced considerably in mapping out an original road to socialism and had begun to do so in the period between the two wars, after the Seventh Congress of the Communist International. We were talking earlier, you remember, about the elaboration of the prospects for a new type of democracy, for progressive democracy. For his part, Gramsci in prison had done inspired work on the themes of the search for a road to socialism different from that travelled in Russia; during the 1950s his *Prison Notebooks* had begun to become part of the heritage of the Party cadre. Of course, then many aspects of his thought and of his political experience had not yet been openly confronted and neither had the relations between his thought and that of the Party where they differed. Well, when the Twentieth Congress of the CPSU presented us with the opportunity to vigorously resume the interrupted search, to render consistent a whole series of our positions, including theoretical ones. The leadership of the Italian party did not hesitate to seize this opportunity. We confronted quite fundamental questions: the question of a socialist regime based on a multiparty system, based on the recognition of the autonomy of the various forces of civil society; the question of a new relationship between the Party and the unions, between the Party and the mass organizations, of the need to recognize the autonomy of these organizations even in the process of the building of socialism. At the same time, we clarified our relationship to democratic institutions and liberties. We talked about liberties which could not correctly be called bourgeois because of the role which the working class in countries like ours had in the conquest and consolidation of these liberties. We spoke of the possibility of putting an end in part— and in large part in the present phase — to the illusory character of bourgeois democracy. We spoke of the need to "correct" certain things in the way in which Lenin had presented the problem of the destruction of the bourgeois state apparatus, the problem of the dictatorship of the proletariat.

**H.** *When was this discussed?*

**N.** In 1956, in the report presented to the Central Committee in preparation for the Eighth Congress of the PCI. At the Congress we defined a whole body of positions in such a way as to eliminate any ambiguities in the relationship between our struggle for democratic development and our vision of the building of socialism. We wanted to dissipate the belief that our party intended to proceed along the line of collaboration with other political forces and only respect the rules of the democratic game until such time as it became necessary to make the "leap" toward the establishment of the dictatorship of the proletariat and the building of socialism, after which, on the contrary, the development of the historical process and of our policy would become ever more similar. That had been the experience of the dictatorship of the proletariat and of the construction of socialism in the Soviet Union. Did we believe this or not? We frankly faced the question and removed any ambiguity. We clarified our conception not only of the advance to socialism but also of the building of socialism, and our conception of the relationship between democracy and socialism as one of substantial continuity.

**H.** *But in doing so, didn't you run the risk of creating other misunderstandings? That is, if one foresees a transition to socialism which passes through bourgeois democracy in an infinite series of steps, how does one avoid falling into a Social Democratic conception? In short, what about the question: Wasn't the PCI beginning to turn itself into just another reformist, gradualist party, into a new type of Fabianism?*

**N.** We have worked on these problems since 1956, and we still work on them. We must continually clarify our positions and remove any old and new misunderstandings.

In his report to the Tenth Congress at the beginning of 1963, Togliatti said frankly that our vision of the advance toward socialism includes the concept of a *gradual* development. I think that in reality the point that distinguishes our conception from the traditional theory and practice of social-democratic parties is not whether we accept or do not accept the concept of gradualness. I am convinced that the basic difference lies elsewhere: It is whether one truly has or has not a vision of advancing toward socialism and building socialism, with all that that requires in theoretical work, in a struggle of ideas, in a rigorous appraisal of the experiences of socialist construction and struggle for socialism in the world with all that that requires in the choice of sides on the international level. I don't mean identification with a military-political bloc but rather a consistent attitude of struggle against imperialism, of developing internationalist ties with the people's liberation movements and with the struggles for effective economic as well as political independence on the part of peoples of vast areas of the world. I am convinced that the difference lies also in the conception of the steps to take, the reforms to win, the ways to develop democracy, because this can be part of a line of advance toward socialism. As far as we are concerned, what we are trying to do is to give ever newer and richer content to democracy—promoting an effective mass participation in the management of economic, social and political life, transforming economic and social structures, carrying out substantial changes in the power relationships between the classes.

**H.** *The transition to socialism can be a very long process, with many ups and downs, compromises, etc. But the classical school, if I can use the expression, has always considered the change, the*

*transfer of power, to be an important moment—even if this is not
necessarily done in the manner of the October Revolution.*

**N.** I mentioned that one of the elements which characterizes
our conception is precisely that of a change in the power relationships between the classes. This means seeing if this change
can itself come about gradually. I am convinced that it can, on
the basis of the experience we are going through. There is no
doubt that in the last five or six years Italy has seen a growth in
the political influence of the working class and of its capacity to
intervene in the economic, social and political life of the country,
even regarding those decisions with the greatest influence on the
general course of development of the country. Today the problem of a change of the governing class is on the agenda, at least
and above all in the sense of acknowledging an adequate place in
government for the working class, for the working masses. We
can thus imagine a more or less long period of transition, during
which forces representing in the broadest manner the working
class and forces representing other classes would coexist in the
government of the country. We can hypothesize the concrete
manifestations at the governmental level of a growing influence
of the working class—of the laboring classes—on social and political life and at the same time the continuation of the development of the dialectic and struggle for hegemony between antago-
nistic social forces. The construction of socialism, of course,
entails the full leadership of the working class and of its allies;
this is still an aim as we move through such a process.

You see, from 1956 (I cannot get away from that turning
point), we have been ever more clearly elaborating a conception
of the revolution as process, as the process of the progressive affirmation of the working class as a ruling class, through a struggle conducted on various fronts for the hegemony of the working
class towards and in confrontation with other classes. Frankly,
all this seems to me to have very little to do with the traditional

conceptions and practices of social democracy. It seems to me that ours is truly an original vision—or search, if you will —corresponding to all the experience which we have accumulated as a Communist Party and as a workers' movement, in Italy as well as outside of Italy. This is the discussion that we started in 1956; and it is still going on.

**H.** *How did this discussion develop after the death of Togliatti and in relation to the events in the international Communist movement?*

**N.** The debate inside the international Communist movement had opened even before the death of Togliatti. The Yalta memorandum is clear testimony of the Italian Communist Party's efforts to place itself in an autonomous position with respect to the divisions—the most serious and deepest of which was that which exploded between China and the Soviet Union—and before the problems of the Communist movement. Other facts arose (above all, the events of Czechoslovakia) which dramatically forced on the PCI leadership the need to deepen and develop even further our own vision of socialism, of the relationship between democracy and socialism, of the problems of the socialist world and of the worldwide revolutionary and workers' movement.

This was a serious moment for us; we must not forget how crucial was the decision that we had to take in the hours immediately following the military intervention of the Soviet Union and of the other Warsaw Pact countries in Czechoslovakia, how crucial for us was the formulation of a document in which we openly expressed our serious disagreement with that intervention. Hence, the Central Committee prepared, with Longo's report, a full explanation of our disagreement. In the months following, the problems stirred up by the military intervention in Czechoslovakia were closely tied to those of a further autonomous development of our line of advance toward socialism. This was the meaning both of the Twelfth Congress—the one held in Bologna at the beginning of 1969—and of our subsequent line in respect to the worldwide conference of Communist parties and during that conference. As far as the relations between the Communist parties and the prospects of the Communist movement are concerned we carried out decisively the line of unity in diversity.

**H.** *Could I turn to another subject: the problem of party cadres? In the 1950s and 1960s major changes took place. At what point did the generation of the Resistance—that is, your generation—begin to become the national leadership? Before Togliatti's death?*

**N.** Yes, before Togliatti's death, starting with the Eighth Congress (1956) which saw the entry of many militants of that generation into the Central Committee. In the course of subsequent congresses, they also gradually made themselves felt in the leadership of the Party. This was essentially not a simple (you might say biological) process of generational change, but the outcome of a battle to renew the Party begun before 1956 and which had culminated, in many provincial organizations, in many federations, with the preparations for the Eighth Congress. Even today, twenty years afterwards, we can see this battle as the determining factor effectively winning over the Party to the major strategic choice of the Italian road to socialism, eliminating what has been called "duplicity" in the orientation and behavior of the Party. This battle was a guarantee to all that our words and actions agree. In fact, it is not enough for a leading group to elaborate and enunciate a line. The Party is a living organism, and if it is not fundamentally convinced of the correctness of that line—by means of a democratic discussion and, if necessary, a deep political struggle—if its leading forces are not renewed at the correct moment, because the consistent development of the adopted line requires it, then sooner or later contradictions arise which must be paid for.

**H.** *It seems to me that there were no substantial divergences within the leading group on the international line as developed by Togliatti from the Twentieth Congress to the Yalta memorandum. Am I mistaken?*

**N.** No, you're not mistaken; where there were reservations was at the middle level of the Party.

**H.** *However, after the death of Togliatti, disagreements did develop—even inside the leading group—on internal policies though they were later settled. Could you say something about this discussion?*

**N.** It was a complex discussion. It may, perhaps, seem difficult to comprehend today (I am speaking of that discussion which erupted at the Eleventh Congress of the PCI, held in the beginning of 1966), but it was certainly indicative of the difficulties which faced our Party and the Italian workers' movement in those years. Furthermore, the discussion was sharpened by the concern which many of us felt right after the death of Togliatti: the need to consolidate and not to imperil the unity of the Party.

You spoke earlier of the uncertainties which beset the workers' movement—not only in Italy—during the long period of the capitalist and especially of the European capitalist boom. I would even say perspectives were lost or dimmed. Toward the end of the 1950s, a symptomatic debate began among the European left on the tendencies of neocapitalist development, which seemed to refute the predictions of Marx and the Marxist doctrine. Even in the middle of the 1960s, there was a lively, a tormented debate on the perils of "integration" of the working class into the capitalist system, of subaltern adaptation of the working class to the "rules" of the system and to the models of behavior suggested by the ruling classes. On the political level, moreover, there really was a maneuver aimed at locking a part of the workers' movement, represented by the Socialist Party, into a subordinate and binding governmental collaboration. The aim was to split the whole unitary tissue of the workers' movement, from the local administrations to the union organization. The policy of the center-left coalition, begun in 1962 with great ambitions and interesting possibilities, had quickly become a tool of this maneuver.

This was serious and insidious, and it provoked consternation and tension inside our party. When the Eleventh Congress met, relations between Communists and socialists, which had already seriously deteriorated, were getting more and more bitter on the issue of the projected unification of the Socialist Party and the Social Democratic Party.

This complex of developments—the capitalist boom and in Italy the end of the socialist-Communist alliance and the center-left alignment—weighed heavily on us until 1968. It caused a sense of uncertainty and preoccupations about the future. Then came 1968.

**H.** *Are you saying that all these uncertainties and discussions were resolved by history itself, that is, when mass popular struggles revived and became more radical and when the outlines of a capitalist crisis could be seen?*

**N.** Exactly. The break came in 1968, but in Italy 1968 was not only the year of student revolt, of youth protests; it was also the year of a clear move to the left, of a firm success of the PCI in the general elections. That was when the crisis of the center-left coalition and of the unification of the PSI and the PSDI began. The new militant thrust that then came from the working class put the problem of the unity of the workers' movement and of a change in social relations firmly on the agenda.

In 1969, the Socialist Party recovered its autonomy and began to review its political line: A gradual reconciliation between socialists and Communists began.

**H.** *But at the same time there was the formation of a left wing outside the Communist Party. This was new. It seems to me that it expressed criticism of the operation of the historic institutions of the working class. Do you think that this criticism was totally unjustified?*

**N.** What has been called the extraparliamentary left arose not from a criticism but from a radical denial of the leadership capabilities of the parties and other "traditional" organizations of the working class. Naturally there were reasons for criticism, even of a party like ours which had always been in the opposition. It is a patent fact that we had been slow to catch the meaning and implications of the tumultuous growth of the student population, the contradictions that this growth brought with it, the ferments of discontent and of rebellion that were maturing among the masses of students. This was a new social phenomenon, and it provided a sort of mass base for the attack on traditional institutions of the working class. In order to explain the rise of the protest movement we must bear in mind, along with this social fact, the ideological and political fact of the crisis in the global Communist and revolutionary movement: there was the split between China and the Soviet Union, the influence of the Chinese criticisms of parties like ours, the impact of revolutionary "third world" experience and theorizing.

**H.** *How did the Party react to the shock of the student revolt and of the opposition "from the left"?*

**N.** The question is important, and there is much that can be said about it. Between the end of 1967 and the beginning of 1968, we went through a critical period: we were acutely aware of the danger of a break with new forces—especially but not only students—that were moving in a revolutionary direction, even if in confused and often unacceptable forms, and did not identify with our Party, with its political and ideological heritage. Instead they challenged it; they seemed almost beyond our reach. In our ranks there were different reactions, and certainly not all of them were correct: Some tended toward total rejection, some toward excessive concessions. All in all, a line of self-critical investigation prevailed. We tried—without "selling out" our heritage, without demagogically pursuing or taking over as ours the positions that were raised in opposition to us—to analyze the diverse roots and components of the student protests, social, ideological, political or cultural. We tried to see how much influence our own insufficiencies at all levels might have had and to draw conclusions even to the point of correcting certain of our attitudes, of overcoming some of our inertia. By 1971, we had organized a conference on "Marxism in the 1960s" and on the ideological and political formation of the younger generations. We endeavoured to combine self-critical openness, efforts to understand and critical rigor in regard to the character and concrete developments of the movement that had erupted during 1967 and 1968. The results of the 1968 elections already showed that we had succeeded in overcoming the most critical phase and in establishing a relationship with some of the young people who came to prominence during the protests.

**H.** *But is there not more to the protest movement than the student agitation? In the autumn of 1969 in Italy—as in May, 1968, in France—there was an extraordinary and largely spontaneous strike movement.*

**N.** The great strike movement which developed in Italy in the autumn of 1969 cannot in any way be called spontaneous. In 1968 and 1969 the unions had serious difficulties and had to carry out a major effort at renewal, but they fully affirmed their leadership in shaping the struggles of 1969, precisely because they had understood the lesson and the thrust which had come from the young people's protest—the push, above all, for a new democratic relationship between organizations and masses, for more active and direct participation by the workers (especially the younger generations of workers) in the conduct of the struggles. So the protest touched only the fringes and did not penetrate deeply into the working class.

During that period the glorification of the spontaneity of the movement and the radical negation of the strategy and of the role of the "traditional" institutions of the working class—considered, by extremists unredeemably obsolete—led the "Manifesto" group to break with our party. But the facts have demonstrated the inconsistency of those positions: many vague aspirations or expectations of that group, and of other formations of the extra-parliamentary left, fell and gave way to rather different modes of behavior. The line of founding new political and union tools as an alternative to the "traditional" institutions of the workers' movement has had to be abandoned.

**H.** *Can we say definitively that the Party has succeeded in renewing a link with the young people of 1968 and that a new generation has come forward in the Party?*

**N.** Yes, starting with 1969 and 1970, a large part of the youth who had animated the protest movement entered into the ranks of the Youth Federation and of the Communist Party, after a phase of bitter polemics with our party. This tendency continued in the succeeding years. From among these young people, new leading cadres were rapidly selected and promoted. After 1970 the Party went through a process of intense and general rejuvenation; cadres between twenty and thirty were given important responsibilities on the section and federation level.

# II

**HOBSBAWM:** *The end of the 1960s marked an historic turn-ing point. This brings us to the present period, that is, to the crisis of the neocapitalism that had seemed so prosperous and sta-ble in the fifties and sixties. As we have agreed, social tensions were the first symptoms of this crisis.*

**NAPOLITANO:** Yes, the exceptional breadth and combativ-ity of the movements during 1968 and 1969 can be explained by the explosion of social contradictions within the process of eco-nomic development before the actual crisis of that type of devel-opment itself had broken out.

**H.** *I think we've reached the point where we can discuss the present-day situation, which is once again a situation of capital-ism in crisis. First, would you agree that the present crisis is not the same as that of the 1930s, even though it has some similari-ties?*

**N.** I don't think anyone can deny the exceptional depth and complexity of the present crisis of the capitalist world. But I don't want to make a partial analysis of this crisis—as seen from the point of view of our country, of the workers' movement in our country. Suppose I throw the question back at you, since you can speak from a point of view which is not narrowly Italian. Seen from a broader vantage point, how does it seem to you that one can define this crisis? Will you permit this momentary role reversal?

**H.**   *With pleasure, but—as you well know—it is rather difficult to define the current crisis. I would say that we are certainly at the end of an historical period of capitalist expansion, which does not mean capitalism cannot recover. Perhaps this crisis can be compared to the so-called great depression of the late nineteenth century. You remember, though the production indices were rising, there were certain difficulties in the capitalist economy for decades, and the mass workers' and socialist movements developed during these years. Today, we are not necessarily in a catastrophic crisis like the one of 1929–1930. Perhaps it would be premature to say more than this, but if we agree on the fact that we are at the end of an historical epoch of capitalist expansion, we can discuss some possible positive and negative consequences of this. How does that strike you?*

**N.**   I think we have to be careful neither to envisage the probable evolution of the present crisis of the capitalist world in catastrophic terms, nor to underestimate the gravity and unprecedented character of this crisis. Some people have compared this crisis with 1929–1930, but this is unconvincing, for many reasons. Still, it is a fact that we are not simply faced with a cyclical fluctuation of the traditional kind. Just consider the significance of some manifestations and implications of the current crisis: there is a crisis of the monetary system, a crisis of international economic relations, tensions in the relations between capitalist countries—between the different areas of the capitalist world, between the United States and other countries or groups of countries, between the United States and Western Europe—and tensions in the relations between developed capitalist countries and countries of the third and fourth worlds, as they are now called. There is the dramatic and in a sense unique oil crisis and the conflict that has arisen between the third world petroleum-producing countries and the developed capitalist countries. However, tensions are also developing on a much wider front, namely between the backward and developing countries as a whole in relationship to the countries of the capitalist West. Finally, the problem of the prospects for collaboration between the capitalist world and the socialist countries assumes new aspects. All these areas are disturbed; in all these spheres there is today a difficult search for new equilibriums, it would be very difficult and entirely premature to predict its outcome. This is the framework into which we must set specific elements of the Italian crisis. I would say that our national vantage point allows us to see with particular clarity the multiform character of this crisis of capitalism. We see it not only as an economic crisis but also as a social and political crisis, a crisis of the capability to lead, of the hegemony of the old ruling classes.

**H.** *This last point is rather important. It seems to me that the possibilities of right-wing or reactionary solutions to the crisis are dimmer now than in the early 1930s; almost everywhere the workers' movement is better organized, more combative, and the ruling classes are weaker. On the other hand, it is hard to believe that in the course of such a crisis of the capitalist system there will not be attempts to attack the working class, especially in those areas where it has advanced furthest. Do you think that the movement in Italy and also in other parts of Europe is strong enough to resist them? Can it utilize this political, social and economic crisis to come out stronger than before?*

**N.**   Before answering with a simple yes, which could also be a sign of overly facile optimism, I would like to say that I am also convinced that the difficulties for a right-wing, authoritarian and even fascist-type response are much greater for the ruling classes today than in other historical epochs. However—and perhaps this view reflects those peculiarities of the Italian Communist Party which we have been trying to explore since the start of our conversation—we are so marked by the historical experience of the defeat of the workers' movement by fascism that we believe in never underestimating the possibilities of right-wing solutions. We must always pay attention to the danger of the creation of conditions for the development of reactionary offensives or counteroffensives by the ruling classes.

Since 1969, we have had in Italy simultaneously a working-class and left-wing offensive and advance, a broad political and economic movement of the working class and attempts at reactionary offensive in the form of what has been called the strategy of provocation and tension and also in the form of the most brutal terrorism. We came out of it all right, because we both reacted firmly to the dangers of intimidation and disorientation that the strategy of terror might have caused and worked to avoid the creation or consolidation of a mass base for a right-wing movement in opposition to the working-class advance. It seems to me now that in the current stage of acute and complex social crisis, and of a serious political as well as economic crisis, we must consider the possibility that a wide and varied social bloc might be formed around a right-wing line in opposition to the workers' movement. How might this maneuver, this counteroffensive, develop? I think above all we must take into account the fact that the cancerous spread of the economic crisis can push a part of the middle classes to the right.

**H.**   *For example small farmers and small businessmen.*

**N.** Particularly the small and medium-sized industrialists who feel heavily the pressure of the workers' demands, the weight of the higher cost of labor, and who are placed in a rather difficult position by the conditions of a market dominated by large monopolistic concentrations.

We must also pay attention to the contradictions that can develop inside the laboring and popular masses themselves: between employed and unemployed workers, between the employed workers and the masses of young people—masses which are growing, especially among unemployed high-school and university graduates—also contradictions between industrial workers and employees of the state and of public enterprises or between categories of workers on different rungs of the wage and social ladders.

In substance, serious difficulties may arise for both the line of an alliance between the working class and the intermediate strata and for the working class's policy toward the capitalist forces—its object must be to impede their unification around reactionary positions—as well as difficulties for the very unity of the working class and of the laboring masses. This is the point where a right-wing, antidemocratic maneuver can intervene, though it is difficult to say what precise character it might take. However, thanks to the powerful revival of antifascist consciousness and action which has taken place in the last few years in Italy, it would certainly not be easy for a right-wing maneuver to assume the form of an openly fascistic movement.

**H.** *I think it is easier to isolate the neofascist forces than to solve the contradictions which can develop within the working classes and popular masses since unemployment and inflation affect different sectors in different ways.*

**N.** So you also believe that the simultaneous presence of unemployment and inflation can cause very difficult problems for the working-class movement?

**H.** *Yes, I am sure it can. How does the PCI see this very serious and concrete problem?*

**N.** In Italy the workers' movement has succeeded in winning some important weapons for the defense of the standard of living of the employed workers faced with inflation or with temporary crises of firms or productive sectors. I am thinking of the institution of the escalator clause, recently brought up to date and perfected, to the winning of the guaranteed salary, etc. Inflation hits other social strata harder, starting naturally with the unemployed. We should not—this should be clear—neglect action for an even more efficient and integral defense of real wages and for a further improvement of the conditions of employed workers, but it would be a mistake not to give the greatest importance, as a workers' movement, to the defense of the interests of those popular strata and social classes which are hardest hit by inflation, first of all to the defense of the interests of the unemployed and of youth. These are the people who, because of the crisis, are finding it harder and harder to get jobs and secure income.

Another problem is the tendency of the better-paid workers to defend their favored positions. Against this, there is a thrust on the part of the most deprived categories of workers toward a lessening of the differentials between them, toward equalization. In Italy this problem is particularly acute and terribly complicated in the public sector, in the very substantial mass of employees of the state, of public enterprises, of local enterprises. In this sector there is effectively an enormous variety of salary scales, a lot of completely unjustified disparities and inequalities, the result of a policy of particular concessions category by category, group by group (developed in the course of more than twenty years by the rulers and administrators of Christian democracy). This policy has constituted an important element in the building of the Christian democratic power machine. Furthermore, the rising salaries of rather substantial strata of employees in public administration and the public services along with, more generally, the rising incomes of vast ranges of the middle strata was, in fact, one of the bases of the economic development mechanism of the 1950s and 1960s. It contributed notably to the growth of opulent private consumption and to the distortions which have, as we know, characterized Italian economic development.

Getting back to the question I started with and to the point at issue, I think we must manage to reform, reorder and rebalance the pay structure in the sphere of public and service employment. We must establish just and equitable relations between income levels among all the different categories of workers—in industry, in agriculture and in the tertiary sector. Since 1968 and 1969, we have succeeded in winning a notable improvement in the conditions of salaried and industrial workers, and we succeeded in bringing about a global increase in the share of dependent labor incomes in total national income; however, at present there are problems not only in consolidating this tendency but also of redistribution within that share of the national income which goes to income from labor. This problem can be the source of serious difficulties and contradictions for the working-class movement, especially inasmuch as this crisis may revise and strengthen narrow self-interest, what we call a corporative line, with each group looking exclusively after its group interests.

**H.**  *Yes, we must return to Lenin's and Gramsci's critique of "corporativism"; class consciousness is not the same thing as even the most militant esprit de corps.*

*Returning to what you were saying, is it not characteristic of a deep crisis in which total income stagnates or declines that problems of income redistribution and sacrifices arise even within individual sectors? Doesn't it seem to you that here is the heart of the problem of how to move forward and overcome the crisis?*

**N.**  I think that the problems that we have discussed until now can be correctly confronted only in the framework of a policy aimed, as you say, at getting the country out of the crisis. This is certain. Questions of making sacrifices and of a redistribution of income even inside the working classes can be posed only insofar as they are related to the objective of overcoming the crisis along the lines of a profound renewal of the economy and of society. In a time of crisis the privileges of the ruling classes, of the classes that draw profits from the large capitalist enterprises, of the classes tied to speculative income and activities are more visible than usual and indeed magnified. The workers' movement cannot accept a policy in which the government hypocritically proposes sacrifices and equalization only within the working classes and does not touch the positions of privilege.

**H.** *Fine. But what prospects for getting out of the crisis does the PCI see? Might the crisis perhaps be in some part overcome by another period of capitalist development like the last one, perhaps with greater controls on the income of industrialists, speculators and rentiers? Wouldn't this mean accepting a subordinate role for the working class? How can we get out of the present crisis in such a way as to move forward toward socialism? Isn't this a basic question?*

**N.** Yes, it is a basic question. This is exactly what we are looking for: a way of overcoming the present crisis that does not lead to a pure and simple revival of the traditional developmental mechanisms of the capitalist economy, such as were at work in Italy in the 1950s and 1960s. This perspective rests on one fundamental assumption. The working-class movement must be fully aware of the need to give a positive answer to the problems raised by the crisis of capitalism. On various occasions—we have also returned to these questions recently—there have been complex discussions on the way we should interpret the theory of crisis in Marx, on whether we can or cannot speak of a "theory of the collapse" in Marx and in the subsequent development of Marxist thought. I think that the policy of our party is based on the profound conviction that we must not expect a socialist-oriented change to derive from the collapse of a capitalist economy. We must intervene in the crisis of capitalism in such a way as to affirm the leading role of the working class, so as to weld around it a bloc of social forces, a broad system of alliances, giving the country a new political leadership capable of initiating a process of transformation. We must also fight corporativism, the narrow-minded group outlook, which always tends to grow inside the working classes, by making ourselves the bearers of a constructive vision of the function of the working class.

**H.** *Are you thinking of Gramsci here?*

**N.** Yes, Gramsci's inspiration guides us: the Gramsci of "Ordine Nuovo," the Gramsci of 1923–1926, the Gramsci of the reflections on the defeat of the workers' movement, the Gramsci of the *Prison Notebooks*. Nobody has expressed better than Gramsci this constructive vision of the revolutionary function of the working class, the need for the working class to have a constructive attitude when faced with problems of production, the need for the working class movement to show alternatives in the very fields of the organization of production and of the management of the economy. Gramsci wrote in 1924 that for the working class and its movement, seizing the state means, above all, having the capacity to outdo capitalists in the managing of the country's productive forces. Gramsci considered this to be a fundamental area of confrontation and of struggle for hegemony, for the affirmation of the working class as a new ruling class. This is the direction we must take during a period of deep crisis like the present one.

If the workers' movement confines itself to a mere denunciation of the contradictions of the capitalist system and of the responsibilities of the old ruling classes and carries out actions purely in defense of the interests of the workers, then it locks itself into a rather restricted and unmaneuverable position. It isolates itself and gives fuel on the political level to that right-wing maneuver: the reactionary counteroffensive we were speaking of a moment ago. What this attitude supports, in fact, is revival of the capitalist economy on its old bases, however temporary. Or worse still, it may contribute to making the crisis more gangrenous, which can even lead to phenomena such as the disintegration and dissolution of society. This is a real danger. We are very aware of it.

Perhaps you remember the article "Against Pessimism," one of Gramsci's most tormented and dramatic, in which he speaks of the years in which the defeat of the workers' movement and the victory of fascism were ripening. We Communists ourselves were, he said, without wanting it, a factor in the general dissolution of Italian society. I think that what the workers' movement should keep firmly in mind is the need and possibility of our being, in these periods of deep crisis of capitalism, not a factor of dissolution but instead a factor of reconstruction and renewal of society along lines that can open the road to its transformation in a socialist sense.

This is the critical and political premise of the PCI's search for a way to get Italy out of the crisis in conjunction with other working-class and democratic forces.

**H.** *What are the concrete proposals of the PCI on this subject? We agree that the crisis of capitalism is not necessarily resolved in favor of the workers' movement. We have had the historical experience of the 1930s, when the right benefited from the crisis. What is difficult to see, though, is how to get out of the crisis in such a way as to be able to advance toward socialism. For example, in the thirties a workers' movement like the Swedish one helped its own capitalism to overcome the crisis. I would not wish* *to underestimate the achievements of Swedish society, but would such a Swedish perspective satisfy the Italian workers' movement?*

**N.** The first thing to consider is that in our opinion it is impossible to bring Italy out of the crisis and to initiate a lasting development of the Italian economy on healthier and more solid bases without introducing qualitative modifications in the type of development and in the direction of society and of the state. So we do not abstractly proclaim the goodness or superiority of socialism. If we want to aim not for a temporary and illusory revival that will aggravate all the distortions and contradictions of development in the 1950s and 1960s but for a perspective of continual, organic and balanced development of the Italian economy, then we need to introduce "elements of socialism," to use Enrico Berlinguer's expression. We need to implement modifications in the mechanism of development and direction of the economy and society that go in the direction of socialism.

I must add immediately that we do not confine ourselves to the national scene. We are well aware of the importance of problems of foreign demand, of Italy's economic and commercial relations with the rest of the world and of the question of a new international economic cooperation. We are convinced that we must forcefully pose the need for a new place for Italy in the international division of labor. We believe that this is already an acute need. The position that Italy held in the past is no longer sufficient. It is essential to redesign Italy's production for the foreign market; there is an essential need for a new development of Italy's economic and commercial relations with the countries of the third and fourth worlds.

At this point, you would perhaps like to return to the discussion of the new type of development that has to be initiated inside the country.

**H.** *Yes. Could you say something about this?*

**N.** One focus of our discussion is the need to change the emphasis from a forced, artificial and distorted development of private consumption to the development of social consumption. We must satisfy large collective needs, such as the development of public housing, the reform and development of health services, the development and improvement of public transportation, the development and modification of educational structures. At the same time, we point out the need to emphasize productive factors which have been seriously sacrificed until now, like agriculture and agricultural industrialization, essential sectors—like capital goods production—which would also help industrialize the South. In fact any sectors that can contribute along with a strong development of scientific and technological research to a qualitative leap in Italy's productive structure and in Italy's position in the international division of labor should be emphasized.

**H.** *All this is very useful and positive . . .*

**N.** But what does it have to do with the advance to socialism?

**H.** *That's just what I wanted to ask you.*

**N.** The answer to that question is not as easy as it might seem. This might be part of the answer. The social goals of the new development policy that we propose as a way out of the crisis are high employment, the emancipation from backwardness and misery of broad masses of people in the Southern regions, moving the entire national community to a better, more civilly and culturally advanced way of life, no longer distorted and alienating. Does all this have nothing to do with socialism, with the goals of a process of transforming society in a socialist sense?

Even more important is the consideration that the new type of economic development we are thinking of cannot be carried out without important changes in the economic and social structures, in the power relations between the classes and in the state organization itself. I am referring to a whole series of reform measures that are an indispensable condition for the initiation of a new development policy: reform measures in the countryside toward the development of new productive and market structures; reform measures in the cities, for a different way of using the factory areas; reform measures in industry. In Italy, at this point, we are not essentially faced with the problem of new nationalizations, since we already have a sector of public property—in the form, above all, of state participation—more extensive than in any other capitalist country. We are, however, faced with the need to make profound reforms precisely in this public industrial sector so that it will correspond not to behavioral criteria typical of large monopolistic private industry but to the needs of the community, to the directions of a new development policy. I am also thinking of a whole series of modifications to be made in the structure and functioning of the state machinery, aiming fundamentally at decentralization, developing regional and local autonomy, popular participation and control.

More generally, I would like to say that the initiation of the new type of development that we are proposing as an alternative to the attempt to resurrect the old mechanism of expansion is part of the affirmation of a conscious direction of the entire process of economic and social development in the interests of the community. What we are proposing as a way out of the crisis is a broad reconversion of the productive apparatus as part of a new vision of the needs of the country and of Italy's participation in international exchange and in the international division of labor and, therefore, a regulated, strongly programmed and directed development of the future course of economic and social life. We are counterpoising this outlook to the experience of the chaotic, tumultuous expansion of the 1950s and 1960s. We point to these needs as a condition for overcoming the impressive mass of accumulated contradictions and imbalances.

Well, when we speak of conscious direction of economic and

social development, I think that we are speaking of an element that is proper and fundamental to socialism, above all in the sense of overcoming—to use a classical expression—the anarchic character of capitalist development.

**H.** *What you have said is, I think, that in Italy there is a specific situation, characterized on the one hand by a major crisis in the hegemony and capacity to govern of the old ruling classes and on the other hand by the existence of certain instruments for a new planned direction of the economy, which have not yet been used for this purpose. But I ask myself whether it is not dangerous to argue that there is no way out of the crisis without a substantial change in the leadership of society. In the past Communists frequently committed the error of maintaining that there is no way out besides socialism, that capitalism cannot overcome its crises. It was able to do so in the past, and it may be able to do so yet; the problem is one of choosing between differing solutions and not immediately one of the alternative between socialism and catastrophe.*

**N.** You are perfectly right to ask for a clarification of this point. I would like to specify that I am convinced that the problem of conscious direction and regulation of economic and social development, as well as of scientific and technical progress, is a great problem of our epoch on the international level, tied both to the future of the peoples of immense areas living in backwardness, misery and hunger and to the very fate of humanity, menaced today by an ever graver alteration of the ecological balance, of the relationship between man and nature. But I do not draw from this the conclusion that the choice is "socialism or catastrophe." I do not say that the only solution lies in implementing in a short period of time, in some unknown way, socialism on a universal scale. I—or rather we, as Italian Communists— say something different. We are saying that what is necessary is world-wide cooperation and that the element which is itself typical of and proper to socialism—a conscious direction of economic and social development—can be implemented through international cooperation in which backward and developing countries would have a large influence, to which the socialist countries would contribute importantly and in which even the developed capitalist countries would have a place and function.

As regards Italy, I would like to clarify similarly that we do not exclude the existence of possibilities for an economic revival without substantial modifications in the shape and leadership of the country, but we do think that in such a case the revival would be temporary, characterized moreover by an intensification of capitalist exploitation and by an aggravation of all the imbalances of the society. Furthermore, the Italian crisis is not just economic but social, political, institutional and even one of ideas and morals. To overcome a crisis of this nature and to heal the structural weaknesses of our economy it is certainly necessary to change profoundly the direction of society and of the state. We do not, however, conceive of this in terms of a working-class "conquest of power" and a rapid transition to socialism but in terms of an effective accession of the laboring classes into social and political leadership and in terms of the introduction of certain elements proper to socialism in the functioning of the economy and of society. The most important of these elements is precisely programming, or planning the economy, and the participation of the working class, occupying a determining position, in planning decisions at all levels from below and from above. In this context, we do not deny private initiative, much less the function of small enterprises which, in our opinion, have a role to play and a place even in the prospect of socialism; but we concretely assert that the collective interest must prevail in the determination of the direction of the country's economic and social development.

**H.** *Yes, any program on how to overcome the crisis must lay great stress on the social aspect of the working class's participa-*

*tion in a determining position in decisions fundamental to the development of the economy and of society. This is very important.*

**N.** Certainly, we are not talking about a purely technical effort to plan the economy. An economic program aimed at renewal, which is efficient but not coercive is inconceivable without a major social and political mobilization of the working class, laboring and popular forces.

In Italy we have had one experience: that of the economic program tried by the center-left in the 1960s. This was a total failure in substance, because it met with the radical resistance of large capitalist groups to accepting any form of effective public control, any form of discipline coming from the public powers. Instead the policy of the center-left governments depended precisely on the peaceful collaboration of the big capitalist groups. We are today convinced that if we want to carry out the necessary, difficult effort to reconvert the productive apparatus, to reorganize economic and social life as a whole on new bases, it is necessary to initiate a policy of effective economic planning. We know that this policy cannot go forward except in terms of a fighting confrontation with the big capitalist groups, in terms of limiting their decision-making powers and giving the laboring classes adequate powers to intervene in decisive questions of the direction of development. It will be necessary to create, more generally, a new framework of political participation and functioning of the state, to multiply the forms of participation on the part of workers and of citizens generally in the process of decision-making, to multiply the forms of rank-and-file democracy and the possibilities of control from below. Actually, in Italy in the past few years there have been important developments and concrete experiences in this direction.

**H.** *We return again to the specific nature of the Italian crisis, which is fundamentally a crisis of hegemony as revealed by the failure of an entire system of government.*

**N.** I think this is a correct definition of the Italian crisis. But the fact that there is a profound crisis in the hegemony of the old ruling classes means neither that they have totally exhausted their hegemonic possibilities nor that they are ready to abandon their dominant positions peacefully and to accept the hegemony of the working class. Nor does it mean that the working class has succeeded in establishing a consolidated hegemony over sufficiently broad social strata. On the one hand, we see the serious crisis of hegemony of the ruling classes; on the other hand, there is doubtlessly an ever more considerable assertion of the hegemony of the working class over other social strata. The struggle is still in progress. I would say that there is still a no-man's land between these two forces struggling for hegemony. We must not underestimate the fact that the most advanced groups of Italian capitalism are aware of the importance of this struggle; we must not underestimate the efforts that they may undertake. After the June 15 elections, Giovanni Agnelli, President of Fiat and of the General Confederation of Industry, made a symptomatic statement along these lines. he said explicitly: "We are faced with the attempt of new social forces to assert their hegemony. The stakes are high for all concerned."

**H.** *One last clarification. When you say "hegemony of the working class," how do you define the working class—in the classical sense of the manual laborer in big industry? The term is not clear as it was fifty years ago.*

**N.** First of all, when we use this expression we must be careful not to give the impression that we believe in or take for granted a homogeneity of the working class, above all at the level of an ideological and political class awareness. We are well aware of the fact that in a certain sense there is above all a struggle for a hegemony *inside the working class.* We must always work and fight for the working class or—more modestly and concretely— the broadest strata of the working class, its majority, to be fully aware of the majority's historic role, of the leading function that awaits it. This is said to avoid even the implication of some simple fantasizing on our part. I think that we must speak of the working class in a broader sense than in the past, that is, not only referring to manual laborers producing surplus value, but also to other strata of workers, whose objective placement in the productive process is very close to that of the working class and whose level of social and political consciousness makes an effective connection with the working class easier.

Finally, we have always believed that the hegemony of the working class can only be asserted and carried out through its organizations: first of all, the parties of socialist inspiration (certainly not only the Communist Party). Even this problem is more complex today. We feel these must be the guarantee of a dialectical relationship between the political organizations representing the working class and forms of direct expression and participation of the broadest strata of the working class. We must, moreover, be clearer in the sense of not limiting the discussion to those parties. Has the union movement not made an original contribution to the fulfillment of the leading role of the working class? And must we not look more carefully at the contribution that may come from Catholic organizations that by now consider themselves to be part of the workers' movement?

# III

**HOBSBAWM:**  *Let us discuss the international context of the present crisis: How far does it limit the possibility of a strictly national solution?*

**NAPOLITANO:**  In the first place, we cannot think in terms of protectionist or autarchic solutions to the Italian economic crisis—solutions which ignore Italy's need to maintain full relations with other economic areas and especially with the advanced capitalist bloc, within which Italy is situated. This means that the obligations of the balance of payments cannot be escaped. The problem can be approached in very different ways. One way is to consider Italy's present state of inferiority as if it were an immutable condition. Every time the deficit reaches crisis proportions, one resorts to restrictive measures which obstruct any new policy of development on the grounds that the balance of payments does not permit change. There is, however, an alternative possibility. This involves correcting the domestic causes that aggravate the deficits in foreign payments—the structural and productive insufficiencies of our agriculture, the expanded consumption of imported goods, the flight of capital—and seeking to strengthen Italy's international presence and initiative.

**H.** *What, precisely, does this alternative involve?*

**N.** I have already mentioned the need to redesign our export pattern to achieve more advanced positions within the international division of labor and to strive for new and ever more intensified economic and commercial relations with underdeveloped and developing nations. And this—together with the full and rational utilization of national resources in the context of a program of national economic and civic renewal—is the only way for Italy to emerge from the crisis. It is futile to rely on the possible recovery of the American economy, as do some groups in Italy, in the hope that a general improvement in the capitalist economies, including the Italian, will ensue. We do not believe in the validity of such a hypothetical recovery on the same unstable basis as in the past, which in any case placed the Italian economy once again in a marginal and subordinate position. Besides, we think that this time the economies of Western Europe might not benefit at all from an eventual pickup in the American economy. Italy must prepare itself to withstand both American maneuvering to shift the weight of the world crisis onto other countries, including those of Western Europe, as well as the trend towards heightened competition and conflict among European capitalist countries themselves.

**H.** *What is the role of the European economic community in this context?*

**N.** The community has been subject to the negative developments which I just mentioned and is undergoing a profound crisis. Yet the community could well serve as a spokesman for Western Europe's vital need for economic independence; it could favor an autonomous and coordinated development and support a common resistance to the threat that the present phase of the world crisis will lead the United States to reaffirm and strengthen its supremacy against the countries of capitalist Europe. This is the line for which we fight within the EEC. This requires, on the one hand, a substantial turn towards the developing countries, relations of cooperation with all countries on the European continent and initiatives towards the construction of a new international economic order. On the other hand, it also requires a democratization of the structures and orientations of the European economic community.

**H.** *It is not easy to see the prospects within the EEC for a transformation of this kind.*

**N.** The difficulties are certainly enormous. In view of the deepening general crisis of the capitalist economies and the competition among the countries of the EEC themselves, Italy necessarily has to come to grips with the problem of defending its own national interests and developing its own independent initiatives in the field of international economic relations. It is essential at the same time to work tenaciously for a new policy within the European economic community that will enable it to assume a leadership role that no single state can undertake on its own. Incidentally, it should be stressed that even within the ruling groups of the European community, there are positions that are critical and intolerant of the United States' hegemonic pretensions and high-handed maneuvers—regarding monetary policy, commercial relations, etc. Nor should the influence exercised by left-wing forces in the European parliament be underestimated, nor the pressure which can be brought to bear by the trade unions and other popular organizations as they succeed in making themselves felt in the activities of the EEC and in the formation of its policies.

**H.** *You know, of course, that there were great debates in my country about joining the Common Market and that the left took a negative stance.*

**N.** The Italian left, however, was and still is optimistic about England's entry into the Common Market because of the influence which the labor movement has in your country and the contribution toward strengthening the more progressive positions within the Common Market which should result from England's presence. Notwithstanding its present crisis, we are convinced that the EEC is, for all practical purposes, an irreversible reality and, therefore, that every effort must be made to guide its development in a positive way. The need for economic integration among the countries of this area of the world has to be taken into account and acted on in a democratic and progressive fashion, while those dangerous tendencies that escape the authority and control of individual states have to be rigorously controlled; among these, first and foremost, is the expanding power of the great multinational corporations. The left-wing forces and the workers' organizations within the European community must act accordingly. But let us not fall prey to facile illusions. We can see, for example, how difficult it is to coordinate the trade unions' struggles against the multinationals and their efforts to influence the policies of the European economic community. Nevertheless, this is a road along which—however slowly—we can and must proceed.

**H.** *Do you not think that obstacles might arise from within the institutions and policies of the Common Market to the social, structural and political changes that might have to be brought about in particular countries, and especially in Italy?*

**N.** That is one more reason why we are struggling for a democratic transformation of the community.

**H.** *I agree with you when you talk about the impossibility of Italy overcoming the crisis and initiating a process of renewal by* *resorting to protectionism or autarchy. While the first effort to build a socialist economy took place during a period of isolationism in the world economy . . .*

**N.** And in a country like the Soviet Union with its immense size and resources.

**H.** *. . . today the problems of a single country cannot be resolved in isolation. In the last twenty years the opening up and development of world trade and commerce have been immense. This situation means that countries undergoing a process of social transformation are far more exposed to outside economic pressures.*

**N.** But it is also true that in the last forty years a new force has emerged on the world scene, in the form of socialist countries and, among them, a major industrialized nation like the Soviet Union. The relations between the states of capitalist Europe and those of socialist Europe have already become increasingly intensified with the progress of international détente. Further economic, commercial and technical ties with socialist countries might well provide a measure of support for a Western European country engaged in a process of transformation and which, while maintaining organic ties with other countries in Western Europe, is trying to resist external pressures that tend to prevent it from realizing its goals.

Nevertheless, I don't want to underestimate the various pressures and obstacles which could encumber the start of a new type of economic and social development—one that might gradually be capable of being described as socialist—in a country like Italy. At the same time, we can hardly ignore the very rich and complex nexus of historical relations—cultural, political and economic—further strengthened in the last decades which bind us to western Europe. Actually, in many respects they are a characteristic aspect of our view of the democratic and socialist renewal of Italy. In developing our line of action, together with other forces concerned with advancing the process of transforming Italian society, we have to take into account that Italy is in Europe and how this affects our possibilities of action.

**H.** *Do you mean that there is a strong interdependence between the struggle for socialism in Italy and the struggle for socialism throughout Western Europe?*

**N.** Yes. I don't think we should revert to the thesis—which, if I remember correctly, was the focus of discussion in France several years back—of the impossibility of socialism in one country and the resultant need for a simultaneous and coordinated advance toward socialism within all of the nations of western Europe. But there is no doubt that in proceeding in each country toward a transformation of the society in a socialist direction, there has to be a maximum effort to strengthen contacts and reciprocal understandings with the left-wing and democratic forces present and active in the other countries in order to avoid interference or blatant intervention from abroad that would hamper or even interrupt the process of change. More generally, there is a need to act realistically in order to minimize the possibility of pressures and the causes and pretexts for outside intervention.

**H.** *When you talk about pressures and possible interference, are you also referring to the presence of NATO?*

**N.** Certainly. As you know, we are not raising the issue of Italy's unilateral withdrawal from NATO, even if the PCI eventually becomes part of the governing majority. We do not consider this a realistic objective. The real problem is to promote a relaxing of tensions, the effective affirmation of the spirit of détente and peaceful coexistence within each sphere and, in the last analysis, the elimination of Europe's division into military blocs.

**H.** *What are the prospects for this, in your view? And what is your assessment of recent changes in the international situation.*

**N.** The importance of the progress toward détente in international, European and world relations up to the Helsinki Conference for European security and cooperation seems to be indisputable. Particularly indisputable is the importance of the economic and political understandings developed between the United States and the Soviet Union, understandings which constitute an indispensable step in the positive evolution of international relations and the construction of a system of peaceful coexistence. Nonetheless, this process cannot and should not have as its exclusive protagonists the United States and the Soviet Union.

It is inescapable that at the present time there is a growing tendency, especially in the United States, to question the policy of détente as it has emerged over the past few years. The policy might be endangered by developments in the crisis of the capitalist world and of imperialism. The foremost question is, therefore, that of reaffirming and reinforcing the trend toward international détente and peaceful coexistence. This is also the underlying condition for the advance of socialism in a democratic and peaceful way in the western world, in Europe and in Italy. And it is, in addition, the basic condition for minimizing the possibility of outside interference aimed at crushing or obstructing a process of change of the kind for which we are struggling in Italy.

**H.** *What threats are there to détente? A nuclear war between* *the United States and the Soviet Union seems unthinkable. We have now had more than thirty years of world peace, the longest period of peace in this century. But the conflicts among smaller nations strike me as being a very serious danger since they might involve the great powers.*

**N.** I agree that the threat of war presents itself today essentially in the form of local conflicts, in which the great powers are already involved (or risk becoming so). The danger is aggravated by the proliferation of nuclear weapons.

However, I did not have in mind only the extreme case of wars of that character or dimension. I meant to say that we cannot assume that international détente has been achieved, much less that the premises for peaceful coexistence and world economic cooperation have been established satisfactorily and especially insofar as the underdeveloped and developing nations are concerned. Nor can we assume that all threats of a resurgence in international hostilities, including forms of cold war, have been eliminated. We cannot forget that consistent progress towards détente and collective security has been severely limited by the lack of any substantial progress toward reducing armaments levels or of a halt by the great powers in the race for nuclear arms and new weapons of terror and destruction.

**H.** *Certain circles in the United States have expressed considerable alarm about the possible collapse of NATO's political base in the Mediterranean as a result of what happened in Portugal, what might happen in Spain, the turn of events and possible further changes in Greece and the outlook in Italy. You Italians are at the center of American worries.*

**N.** The position we have adopted with respect to Europe and the Mediterranean deserves close attention, for it is not merely a verbal exercise to placate forces (like those responsible for government policy in the United States) that fear the prospect of profound political changes within Europe. It expresses, rather, our own assessment of a number of exigencies and concerns that we hold in need of clarification. I am referring of course to our watch-word calling for a Western Europe that is neither anti-Soviet nor anti-American. We believe it entirely possible to conceive of a Western Europe that is no longer economically and politically dependent on the United States, but that still does not raise the issue of a political rupture or conflict with the United States or the elimination of the United States' economic presence in this part of the world. With specific regard to the Mediterranean, we have adopted a position that takes into account all of the interests involved; it does not call unilaterally for the expulsion of the United States, even if it does seek a solution guaranteeing independence and peace for all of the countries on the Mediterranean.

We realize that certain American groups are obsessed with the fear that southern Europe is about to fall into communist hands. But clearly we are dealing here with an obsession, rather than with a serious political appraisal of the changes which are presently taking place or actually possible in the area of Europe. We hope that there will be a leftward movement within the governments of Southern Europe, but it is absurd for the United States to perceive this possibility in such a catastrophic light.

**H.** *The American economy has proved most resistant of all to the present economic crisis. Generally speaking, there is a tendency to underestimate its strength. But the international position of the Americans is weakening. As a citizen of a country that has lost its empire, I am well aware of the repercussions such a loss can have on domestic politics. The last twenty-five years have been dominated by the American world empire and the United*

*States, both militarily and economically, is still the strongest country in the world. But the international context has changed since the 1950s and is presently undergoing even more profound changes. This could perhaps have a traumatizing effect. How would you assess certain possible American reactions—anti-Communism bordering on hysteria—to the prospect of a further swing to the left in Italy?*

**N.** Although certain changes may be traumatic for the United States, we have to hope that realism and reason will prevail among American political leaders. Historical precedents would suggest this. As for the attitude among certain American groups toward a possible leftward swing in our country's political leadership, it strikes me that in fact there are still incredibly anachronistic and crude images of the Italian Communist Party's policies circulating within official circles and among large sectors of public opinion. But there are also opposing views within the press, the more enlightened cultural circles and liberal political groups; these tend to perceive the policies of the Italian Communist Party for what they are, to deepen their understanding of the undeniable originality and autonomy of this reality. We will do everything we possibly can to respond to requests from American democratic circles to make ourselves better known, to familiarize them with our policies as they really are, without dissembling or embellishment, while at the same time refuting clearly deformed images of our history and our Party's strategy.

**H.** *The problem which comes up again and again in this period of crisis is that of Europe, of the developed nations. In years past, there was a certain tendency toward evasion into "third worldism" among groups committed to revolution. The problem of what is happening in the industrial center of the old world has once more become central, together with the problem of its trans-*

*formation. Nevertheless, this problem cannot be separated from world problems as a whole.*

**N.** I think that it must be said—and we say this with great conviction—that there can be no resolution to the truly dramatic problems facing humanity at the present time—first of all the problem of backwardness, of misery and hunger in so much of the world—unless the advanced capitalist nations totally reorient their policies and place their immense resources, productive capacity, scientific and technical skills and organizational experience in the service of world-wide cooperation. Only in this context will it be possible to guarantee an improvement in the material conditions of existence of people in backward areas, together with the economic and political independence and complete autonomy of development of the countries of the third and fourth worlds. But this means calling into question the present system of relations between the industrialized nations and backward countries—the entire policy of imperialism.

Italy, too, naturally forms part of the bloc of advanced nations in a system of trade relations that continues by and large to perpetuate the condition of exploitation and dependency among the underdeveloped and developing nations. We are struggling, as I indicated earlier, so that Italy's international initiatives take a new direction. As part of this struggle, we are seeking to strengthen the ties of the Italian workers' movement with movements for national liberation and with the present leadership of ex-colonial and dependent nations.

The increased influence of the labor movement, together with a political change in the direction of socialism in the nations of capitalist Europe, correspond not only to the demands of the European working classes and to the urgent need for change which has become so drastically pressing with the current crisis in this area of the world, but also to the interests of peoples and countries of the third and fourth world and to the general concern for peace and progress.

I want to add a final point: The start of this process of transformation toward socialism in the advanced capitalist nations is an essential premise for broadening and renewing the prospects for world socialism to overcome the limits of the experiences in the construction of socialism which have hitherto taken place.

# IV

**HOBSBAWM:** *We haven't talked enough about the question of the Italian road to socialism. Let me ask you, to begin with, what you think of the criticisms of this position from the left.*

**NAPOLITANO:** Those who criticize us at present, who raise objections about, for example, the impracticability of a course of structural reforms, the impossibility of effecting partial structural changes in the economy and society in order to open the way to socialism, who remind us polemically that democracy and the present-day Italian state would in any event conserve their class character, ignore decades of our development and distort our positions. They repeat the kind of dogmatic objections that were first raised by Roger Garaudy, then a leader of the French Communist Party, following our Eighth Party Congress. Yet they take no account of, say, the debates we had with socialist party leaders in the early sixties. At that time, they were the ones who considered the trend toward democratic development in Italy as irreversible—the possibility of advancing toward socialism through the democratic process as having been established beyond all question—and they seemed to underestimate the very real limitations and the potential dangers in the kind of democracy existing in Italy.

We have always believed that the dominant classes may decide at any moment openly to attack democratic institutions and abandon the forms of representative parliamentary democracy. Moreover, we have been consistently aware that the policies of the dominant classes can take an authoritarian turn without the actual destruction of democratic-representative forms. Even at present, we still insist on the fact that the powers of elected and parliamentary bodies are limited and that fundamental decisions for the life of the country lie outside their control. Our vision of political democracy in capitalist countries has never been banally apologetic; on the contrary, it has been constantly attuned to the limitations and dangers inherent in a social and political regime like Italy's. Nonetheless, our only real choice is to surmount the limitations of this democracy, to struggle to give it new forms and a new content—that is economically and socially more advanced—and then to proceed on this basis toward socialism.

**H.** *Nevertheless, choices like the Italian road to socialism raise problems and involve difficulties about which I would like your views. I am thinking of the Chilean experience, not only because of the possibility, which you just mentioned, of the destructive assault by the dominant classes against representative institutions. Insofar as the road to socialism passes over the terrain of parliamentary democracy, it presupposes political alliances and electoral coalitions. The Chilean experience showed the enormous difficulties of translating an electoral alliance into a government capable of bringing about the transformation of the economy and society. Every one of the divergent and particularist interests of the single parties in the Coalition for Popular Unity remained intact after Allende's victory. When I was in Chile, I could see how heavily these interests weighed against resolving such important problems as agrarian reform.*

**N.** Of course we know how complex the problems are which have to be taken into account in advancing toward socialism through the democratic process. We don't think for one moment that we have a ready formula for all of these difficulties, nor do we pretend to have a ready answer for every problem. I want to be very clear on this point. We are engaged in a process. You are quite correct to recall the Chilean experience, because we followed it with immense passion and have continued to reflect on its tragic outcome. Certainly it raises the problem of moving from electoral alliances to popular governments capable of carrying out the process of transformation. But I should say first of all that the effectiveness of such alliances once they become governments depends on the degree of preparedness previously reached by the forces within them. If the left in Italy were to take part in a government today, I believe it would have a far greater chance of success than the alliance between the PCI and PSI would have had in 1948 if the Popular Front had won. Since then, there has been a sustained effort, an accumulation of experiences and occasionally bitter clashes which, in the end, have had the effect of broadening the affinities and points of agreement between the two major parties of the Italian left over the way of understanding the process of transforming Italian society in the direction of socialism. Many aspects are still in need of much further clarification; nonetheless, the understandings already reached represent a reassuring step toward the time when the parties take on together the responsibilities of governing.

If the passage from electoral alliance to government reform action is to be successful, it is equally important that the process of preparation, to which I am referring, should not be confined solely to the top. I am convinced that this process has developed in depth over the past decades in Italy and especially in recent years, penetrating the civic and political consciousness of large masses far beyond the confines of the Communist and socialist electorates. I think, for example, of the recent experiences of trade-union unity and antifascist action and the contribution of the Catholic forces to these movements, of the many forms of democratic participation in governing the cities, the schools and so on, of the powerful political and ideological commitment of the masses and their capacity for organization and self-discipline. All of these, I believe, make our country one of the most mature in its democratic development. I maintain that these developments can play a very positive role in reinforcing effective governmental action by an alliance of popular forces.

But what kind of alliance should we look for? This raises the problem which we Communists raised immediately after the tragic outcome of the Chilean experiment. As you know, at the time Enrico Berlinguer stressed the need to provide Italy with a government and a political direction that were not based simply on an alliance within the left—of the Communist and Socialist Parties—but which had different and far broader bases. This was the premise for the "historical compromise," which has been talked about so much, even outside of Italy.

**H.**  *Right, and in this connection, I want to ask for this: Berlinguer himself observed that the proposition of a "historical compromise" must be conceived not as a mere political alliance, but as a mobilization of a broad range of diverse social groups, going beyond the boundaries of the left. Now, this raises the problem of how a government that represents such a broad social spectrum should act when it is faced with the objective contradictions and conflicts of interest among the social classes and groups to which it is responsible. You yourself mentioned earlier the possibility of such contradictions in referring to the present economic crisis. Naturally, this problem is not unique to the democratic-constitutional road to socialism. We have seen what happened in Portugal; such problems are present in any process of social transfor-*

71

*mation. But what choices should be made? How can any progressive government avoid splits within the major social forces from which it draws support?*

**N.** Let us examine the problem in the context appropriate to the "historic compromise." Suppose we have a particularly broad agreement among all of the currents within the democratic and popular movements, which has been reached—through a convergence of their various positions—for the purpose of providing the country with the strong and authoritative leadership needed to cope with severe problems and carry out the complex process of transformation. In this scenario, it might appear that the problems you raised—about the internal contradictions within the government's social base—would be even more complex than if the government was formed solely by forces of the left. But I don't think so.

It should be stressed from the start that our proposal stems from the conviction that an objective need for profound change in Italian society has emerged as the sole way out of the crisis afflicting the nation and that this need for fundamental renewal is now widespread among the great majority of Italians, not only among the working class and the working population as a whole but also among broad sectors of the middle class. If this were not the case, our hypothesis would not hold. There would, in fact, be no sense in basing the possibility of carrying out this process of renewal on this very broad alliance if a more or less significant segment of these forces represented within it were not favorably disposed to its achievement. We are convinced that such support for a process of transforming Italian society exists, the successive stages and outcome of which will ultimately be defined by the shared experiences of the forces participating in this vast alliance. This prospect does not, of course, eliminate the possibility that in defining the actual content and specific character of reform activity, particular contradictions of a social nature might not arise among the diverse classes and social groups on which the government depends for support. Truly, there are no ready-made answers for such eventualities. It is a question of seeking out the broadest consensus possible around every reform measure and for every change in the pre-existing equilibrium; and for that purpose, a government representing all of the democratic political traditions and ideological currents certainly has a much better chance of success. Moreover, if contradictions within the social base of a reformist alliance arise, we should recall Gramsci's point: that the achievement of the working class's hegemony over other social groups presupposes taking into account the interests and tendencies of those groups and reaching a "certain equilibrium in compromise" with the working class not hesitating to make "sacrifices of an economic-corporative character."

**H.** *You say there are no formulae. I am not certain whether I fully agree with you. Precedents exist; I believe that there is at least one, the attitude of Lenin toward the problem of the alliance with the peasantry. When Lenin saw that the peasants were no longer disposed to follow him, he changed his policies, because he knew that there was no possibility of moving forward without a broad alliance. Even at the cost of halting his own policies, he chose the NEP as the only possible solution. I think that even under very different circumstances the same problem arises of how to combine different classes with different interests around a common program of transformation.*

**N.** You are right to emphasize that there are concrete historical experiences and lessons in method to which we can refer; I meant no formulae in the sense of prefabricated solutions to specific and new problems. Above all, we have to take into account that the problem of working-class alliances in Italy today has to be posed in very different terms even from the way it was posed in our own country thirty years ago, because there have been wholly new developments in social stratification.

**H.** *On this point, I am in complete agreement. In what way do you think that the new social stratification of Italian society has transformed the problem of working-class alliances?*

**N.** In the sense—and this has been true for a long time now—that the problem can no longer be posed solely in terms of the working class's alliance with the peasants or rural semi-proletarians; the fundamental question has become that of all alliances with the non-proletarian strata in the cities which have grown formidably over the last decades in Italy. I am speaking of the alliance with the strata of small and medium-size producers and with those strata of the urban middle class engaged in tertiary activities; above all, I am thinking in terms of the precipitous growth of the ranks of white-collar workers and intellectuals in our country. The masses of intellectuals are themselves extremely composite in character as a result of their diverse relations to the production process, their disparate social functions and their varying levels of income. The problems relating to the non-proletarian urban strata in their entirety are highly complex whether on a theoretical level—as demonstrated by recent debates on the "middle classes" and specifically the white-collar petty bourgeoisie," the definition of which is still extremely controversial—or on the level of the policies which the working-class movement has to develop.

Perhaps the largest question has to do with those groups whose increase has resulted from the abnormal, partly parasitical, partly speculative growth of the cities and to the pathological expansion of certain public sectors. I spoke earlier of the salary differentials among public employees and the phenomena of parasitism and disintegration in the public administration as having become a thorny internal problem for the organized labor movement. It should be clear, in any event, that when we talk about a policy of alliances of the working class, we are talking about a policy that is supposed to change the present state of things and not to consolidate established positions simply for the sake of gaining the support of the intermediate strata in their entirety. We consider it both necessary and possible to win over a decisive part of these groups to the prospect of changing their present condition, to a prospect that is positive and progressive in social and human terms even though, for certain groups, it must necessarily involve the renunciation of certain privileges of an economic-corporative character.

**H.** *I have the impression that we are running two arguments together. We are discussing the question of the Italian road to socialism in specifically Italian terms but at the same time as a much more general problem. The question, therefore, arises: To what extent is the road of advance to socialism, which you are proposing, a purely Italian road, specifically limited to this country?*

**N.** In speaking of an Italian road to socialism, we intended primarily to emphasize our Party's need for and commitment to an autonomous, independent inquiry into the themes relative to the advance toward socialism and the socialist transformation of the society. We wanted to stress the originality of the problems confronting us, as well as their national specificity. It should not be forgotten that we reaffirmed this position after the Twentieth Congress of the CPUSSR which explicitly accepted on the theoretical level the thesis of the possibility of different roads, of national roads to socialism. But today, we cannot avoid taking into account all the matters you and I have been discussing just now, regarding the increasingly ramified ties between Italy and other countries, between the Italian situation and other situations—particularly in capitalist Western Europe. Does this mean that we can no longer speak of national specificity? Of course not. The Italian situation continues to have its own special characteristics and historical peculiarities, which have not been cancelled by the changes undergone by Italian society.

**H.** *Could you be a bit more precise about the specific nature of the Italian situation?*

**N.** In Italy there still exists a Southern question; there still exists a Catholic question. The line-up of political forces is very different from that in other European countries. No other country has a problem similar to that posed by a party of Catholic inspiration, now in profound crisis—the Christian democracy which, while having peasant and popular roots and an antifascist tradition, has acted for the past several decades as a faithful spokesman for the capitalist ruling classes, the big bourgeoisie. We have a socialist party with a strong unitary tradition and a vigorous commitment to the struggle for an effective transformation of the society. I don't want to go on too long with such examples. But we should include among Italian peculiarities the fact that after many years and a lengthy period of schism in the trade-union movement, there is once again a powerful organized labor movement composed of Communist, socialist, Catholic and other elements. There is the fact, too, that our Constitution is far more advanced than those in other countries of Western Europe, to such an extent that in terms of guiding principles and indications for reform it points the way to transformations that are fully compatible with the prospect of an advance toward socialism. There is no doubt that our strategy—the common strategy of the forces struggling for socialism in Italy—has to base itself on all of these peculiarities.

At the same time—as I have already said—we have to take into account a cluster of international relations and pressures that is far denser than twenty years ago; that is the reason why

Italy will not move toward socialism unless the European dimension of the strategy and concrete political initiatives of the PCI and PSI are not strongly developed.

Finally, we have to ask whether certain aspects of our view of the movement toward socialism through democracy, or of the relations between democracy and socialism, have a more general validity outside of the specific case of Italy—whether, in other words, they cannot be considered integral parts of a process of advance toward socialism in other countries of Western Europe. My answer is strongly in the affirmative. It is a fact that in other European countries, too, the Communist parties and movements on the left have arrived independently at theoretical positions and strategic choices similar to those reached by the Communists and socialists in Italy. So, while we should not discount certain inescapable differences and peculiarities, nor claim that all of our views or political and programmatic aims are necessarily applicable to other conditions, we can say that there is and there has to be a common basis for seeking the road of advance to socialism in single countries of Western Europe.

**H.** *Can you be more specific about the underlying common democratic character of the process of advance toward socialism in Western Europe?*

**N.** I think that the fundamental task before us is to affirm working class hegemony through the democratic process. This commitment to constructing socialism necessarily involves several elements which are not only compatible with the goal of carrying out profound structural transformations but are actually indispensable to the renewal and broadening of consensus and to the constant enrichment of the democratic character of the process of building the new society. There must be an appreciation of a plurality of political, ideological and cultural contributions and a recognition of the autonomy of the various manifestations of civil society along with the search for ever more effective forms of participatory democracy and the complete acceptance of principles, such as the respect for the rights of the opposition and the alternation of majority and minority in a parliamentary dialectic. We believe that this is an expression of the organization of democratic life, which must not be abandoned. This evidently implies that ideas which assign to the Communist Party an exclusive leadership role in the process of transforming the society in a socialist direction must be completely and definitively overcome.

**H.** *I will try to be more precise about a point that is not clear to me. What conditions do these countries have in common which make possible or necessary a development toward socialism different from that elsewhere, including in Central Europe? It is also worthwhile remembering that in the third-world countries attempts at multiparty democracy have failed. Are your observations, in any case, restricted to countries with a certain level of industrial development and particular multiparty political and institutional traditions?*

**N.** I believe that in any country the process of socialist transformation as well as socialist regimes have to be founded on a broad basis of consensus and democratic participatation, whatever the specific forms of expression these might have. In this regard, neither the socialist countries nor the third-world nations can be exempted from scrutiny and discussion.

My argument about the principles and forms of democratic life to be upheld in the context of an advance to socialism and the construction of socialist society refers more concretely to the countries of Western Europe in which bourgeois democracy was born, where representative institutions have a more or less strong tradition and diverse democratic, ideological, cultural and political currents have operated more or less freely. These are some of the common points of departure for a socialist transformation in the countries of Western Europe, which, in addition, are characterized in varying degrees—on a structural level—by a complex social stratification, by the presence of sizable intermediate groups between the proletariat and a big bourgeoisie controlling the basic means of production.

**H.** *I am still somewhat perplexed because several different arguments seem to be mixed together in our discussion. First of all, there is the historical element—that is, the reference to the fact that in countries with old bourgeois civic traditions there exists historically civil society with a plurality of parties, a certain kind of intellectual and cultural life and so on. A transformation of, say, Holland or England would be inconceivable without taking these into account. But this historical background has very little to do with the Portuguese case; one certainly cannot speak of a long-time bourgeois-democratic tradition in Portugal.*

**N.** Portugal is by no means the only country in which a reactionary fascist-style regime was instituted in past decades and democratic liberties suppressed for a long time. It happened in Italy and in Germany, in Spain and in Greece, and certainly the historical traditions and democratic precedents of each of these countries could be debated at length. Yet the fact remains that, as soon as these regimes were overthrown, the basic conditions and demand for a democratic public life based on a plurality of contributions and the confrontation among diverse ideological and political currents once more reemerged, and the institutions of representative democracy were restored. Portugal evidently is in many respects a special case: in the way in which the fascist regime was overthrown, the role played by the armed forces in the nation's history and, specifically, in bringing down the regime and, finally, in the functions they assumed under the new government. But in Portugal, too, not by chance, a variety of political forces are now active on the the scene, only some of which played a role in the antifascist struggle, but all now having an impact and the possibility of expressing themselves through the electoral and political process. Not by chance, there was a common agreement on democratic elections and the selection of a representative assembly, even if its tasks were limited exclusively to drawing up the Constitution.

The Communist parties and forces of socialist inspiration in Western European nations are confronted, notwithstanding significant differences, with several important common problems to do with the relation between democracy and socialism. For this reason, we Italian Communists cannot think of closing ourselves off in our own garden, reasoning only about our own problems and defending our line as valid solely for Italy, and then staying silent when critical situations arise in other countries or simply maintaining that everyone can do as they please in their own home. From now on, the choices made by single Communist Parties in Western Europe over the fundamental questions regarding the relation between democracy and socialism directly influence the course of political struggle in other Western European countries as well. Therefore, we do not think we can avoid responsibility for giving our opinion—even admitting the possibility of error from lack of firsthand or thorough knowledge of other situations —by citing positions of principle that are not ours alone and which we hold valid for Communists, no matter in what Western European country they are active.

**H.** *When you speak about positions of principle that are not unique to the PCI, are you thinking about other Communist Parties?*

**N.** I am referring to positions worked out by numerous other European Communist Parties, as well as agreements—on essential points—achieved by diverse left-wing forces in several countries. The French Communist Party elaborated its position auto-nomously, and it then established a working alliance with the Socialists and radical parties to elaborate a common program of government. It reflects problems peculiar to France and to the French left. The political context as a whole is profoundly different from that in Italy. Nonetheless we have seen positions of principle coming out of the common program and the debate within the French left—on the questions of democracy and the relation between democracy and socialism—that are substantially similar to those which we Communists and socialists in Italy sustain.

**H.** *What I wanted to say earlier, however, is that in our discussion, another element, with a social character, has been mixed with the reference to historical traditions in the countries of Western Europe. The need for vast democratic alliances arises perhaps even more from this element, from the fact that the Communist parties, inasmuch as they are parties of the working class, cannot carry out an action of socialist transformation without bothering about the consent, the participation of other classes, of other groups. This held and holds true for Portugal, too, I believe.*

**N.** As far as Portugal is concerned, it seems correct to stress—as others have already done—both the distinctiveness of the Portuguese situation with regard to other Western European countries with more modern and richer social-economic structures and more solid bourgeois-democratic traditions and the impossibility of any simple comparison between conditions in Portugal and those in third-world countries.

The "social" problem, to which you alluded in your question, certainly manifests itself in far more complex terms in the more advanced nations of Western Europe than in Portugal, where the principal problem revolves around alliance with the peasant masses. The focus of discussion, however, is how a specific problem of social alliances expresses and resolves itself in *political terms*. In Portugal, it was possible to believe that support from the peasants and hence from the majority of the population for the process of transformation begun after liberation could be achieved other than through party alliances within the ambit of a system of representative democracy. I refer to the period in which proposals were advanced for an alliance between the armed forces and the people and the development of forms of democracy which circumvented the mediation of parties. The grave social and political laceration which resulted, however, had the effect of endangering any possibility of democratic development and social transformation. Unwarranted or superficial generalizations should be avoided; nonetheless, even the very particular Portuguese situation suggests that certain transitions are obligatory if a transformation in a socialist direction is to take place through the democratic process.

**H.** *Therefore, it is your view that in the countries of capitalist Europe the search for democratic roads to socialism is imperative for reasons inherently to do with both their political-institutional heritage and social character.*

**N.** Yes. But let us look at some of the lessons of history. As you said earlier, proposals for multiparty politics have had no success in third-world countries leaning toward socialism. You also noted that in all of the Eastern and Central European countries taking the road to socialism, the resulting political regimes have differed greatly from the kind which, in our view, should characterize a development toward socialism, a transformation in a socialist direction in Italy and Western Europe. It is true, history tells us, that no successful socialist regime up to now has been established on a plurality of freely competing political parties, in a context in which political liberties are fully exercised and in the broader framework of a highly articulated civil society, of a rich and autonomous dialectic of diverse social, ideological and cultural pressures and positions. We answer that this is still our objective, for history also tells us that up to now neither has socialism in Western Europe been established successfully by means of the Russian road or through models analogous to the Soviet model. This is no accident. The points of departure, the conditions and traditions in each country weigh decisively, as do the historical circumstances and the international context. It is not fortuitous that in those western European countries in which acute (or apparently acute) revolutionary situations arose after World War I, all efforts to seize power following the example of the October Revolution resulted in failure. Socialist transformations were subsequently initiated—in Eastern and Central Europe—even in some countries already developed capitalistically and with considerable bourgeois-democratic traditions (I am thinking of Czechoslovakia); but this happened under historical circumstances which were altogether exceptional and unrepeatable, such as those produced by the end of World War II and its repercussions.

In the light of such historical experience we have concluded that the only path that is realistically open to a socialist transformation in Italy and Western Europe—under peacetime conditions—lies through a struggle within the democratic process, a broadening of the alliances of the working class and its affirmation of hegemony and, finally, a gradual modification of economic and social structures within the framework of a still further development of democracy. This is the only route that corresponds to the complexity of advanced capitalist societies and the political and cultural peculiarities of a country like ours.

For the rest, even if it were possible to affirm the power of the working class and achieve socialism by repressing democratic liberties and the pluralistic traditions of countries such as Italy, we would have to ask the price in terms of building socialism: How much would such a choice affect the character of the socialist society in construction? How far would it be in practice from the conception of socialism as the highest expression—in a real, not a purely formal sense—of the values of liberty and democracy?

**H.** *Don't you think that your observations about what socialist democracy should be are overly influenced by the particular historical and institutional traditions of Western Europe? And that you end up overemphasizing their more general validity?*

**N.** Allow me to answer with a phrase from Togliatti, which strikes me as both beautiful and significant: "The present-day democratic institutions of the West are not the end point of history." They are not so in the sense that democracy has to be further developed. "From democracy we want to take nothing; we want to add to it many things": new forms of worker control and direct participation in the organization of production, autonomous organizations providing for mutual aid and collective control in various fields of civic life that will gradually take over from what is now a suffocating state apparatus.

This is what we want, and it is not a simple declaration of intent. It is pointless to ask continually whether we are really sincere, whether our commitment to safeguarding and developing democracy is not negated by psychological reservations of some kind or to insinuate that it is all a cunning trick to conceal a prearranged coup de main. In the last decades, our Party has contributed to educating millions of people regarding the meaning of liberty, a taste for democracy, the practice of democracy—to engaging millions of people in the struggle to defend and develop democracy. In this way, it has become inextricably tied to the prospect of an advance to socialism through democracy. If we even tried to abandon this path for a moment, we would bring about an irremediable crisis in our relations with the great mass of our followers.

**H.** *Can we now see the discussion of the Italian road to social-ism into a much broader context? For the Italian Communist Party, the problem of a nonrapid transition to socialism is funda-mental, but no transition to socialism is conceivable unless the experiences of socialist transformation which have taken place in the last half century are considered. I don't know whether you are among those who deny the socialist character of these experi-ences, but let us begin with the idea that they should be judged as such. Is it possible, in your view, to draw up a balance sheet, learn lessons, either positive or negative? Without going into the historical circumstances that generated those experiences, are there not teachings to be derived for those engaged in the struggle for socialism?*

**N.** I think we are still too much bound up in the contrast be-tween those who deny the socialist nature of the societies that have been built or are being constructed on the bases of major upheavals in the sphere of the ownership of the means of pro-duction and those, by contrast, who defend the socialist character of such experiences. We cannot become bogged down in such antitheses or elementary polemics. I am of the opinion that it is absurd to deny the socialist nature of the processes of transfor-mation completed over the past half century in Europe and on other continents under the direction of workers and Communist parties. This is not a question of exalting the embodiment—in such societies—of the ideals of socialism in all of their purity and fullness, nor of extracting a kind of optimal model of socialism. The experiences up to now were historically conditioned efforts to build socialism, arising out of certain great national revolu-tions and developing under diverse circumstances and in differ-ent ways with characteristics both positive and negative. It is in-evitable that future experiences will be different since they will be taking place under historical conditions dissimilar to those in which socialism was constructed in the Soviet Union and elsewhere. It is both possible and necessary that the experiences in building socialism in the capitalist West overcome some of the limits, avoid certain of the dangerous negative aspects of the changes in the Soviet Union and other countries. We believe that the fundamental negative aspects lie in the suppression of individual liberties and the limitations imposed on the possibilites of articulating and developing a democratic public life, which in varying degrees and at diverse moments have characterized the experiences of socialist construction in the Soviet Union and elsewhere. By far the most dramatic recognition of the limits and deformations in this area came from the very Communist party of the Soviet Union at the Twentieth Congress, in referring to the Stalinist period. However, the analysis made at that time of the phenomenon of Stalinism or the Stalinist period is highly debatable. So are the attempts subsequently made to overcome not only the worst, most profound deformations of the Stalinist epoch but also the organic limits manifested in the development of socialist democracy.

In essence, the problem lies in further examining the merits of these experiences i.e., we must not confine ourselves either to condemning them en bloc or defending their socialist character. I do not say exalting them en bloc since this attitude has long since disappeared, at least from within the PCI.

**H.** *Is it not true that between your Party militants and the socialist countries, the human and political ties are traditionally strong?*

**N.** We will never be able to forget the significance for the most advanced part of the working class in this country of the conviction that socialism was finally becoming a reality, a shining reality and a guiding light in one part of the world. The effect on the consciences and in the struggles of the most advanced sector of the working class in Italy was extraordinarily fortifying over long periods, and especially during fascism, during the Second World War, right after Liberation and during the years of the Cold War. We cannot ignore the ideological bonds and the feeling of solidarity with the socialist world—with the peoples of the Soviet Union above all—that are so deeply rooted in great masses of our militants and workers. Nor can we accept that the international role of the Soviet Union in the struggle against imperialism and for peace be ignored or denied. But this has not meant, for many years now, that we assume positions that result or even tend to result in an indiscriminate exaltation of existing socialist societies. For years now, we have combined positive and negative in our judgments of these societies. It is necessary, however, that we deepen our historical and critical understanding of such experiences. Italian socialists, too, would be well advised to commit themselves at this level, especially those who pass absurdly summary judgments on the Soviet Union, dismissing the Soviet reality as a police state.

It is necessary to examine further specific aspects that are much debated and problematic, yet characteristic of the historical development in socialist countries, from which lessons might be drawn despite the profoundly different conditions under which a transformation in a socialist direction will take place in Italy and other advanced capitalist nations. I refer, in particular, to the experience with economic planning—such as has been undertaken in various phases and in several countries, beginning with the Soviet Union—for nearly fifty years now. In studying such experiences, I believe, we will come across problems which we, too, will have to deal with sooner or later—problems, I should say, of a theoretical and political nature—that must be confronted in light of the trials and errors, debates, choices and results of the experience in planning in the socialist countries, precisely so that we can be certain to arrive at solutions different from those already attempted. We have not sufficiently developed this inquiry, this effort of critical reflection.

## The Italian Road to Socialism

**H.** *You say definitively that there is no single model for socialism; one has to talk about different models and different modes of transition to socialism. In countries with more advanced bourgeois civic traditions, with a richer bourgeois democratic heritage, there has to be an effort to safeguard fundamental elements of this legacy. This raises an important problem with respect to the dialectic within revolutionary societies. They represent both a break with the past and the conservation of certain elements within it. This is true everywhere. I am convinced that Communist China is very Chinese, just as revolutionary France was very French in terms of its past. How, in your view, would the case of Italy appear in this regard?*

**N.** We are not really talking about different models of socialism but rather about the possibility, indeed the historical need, for new experiences, whether in the transition to socialism or the construction of socialism. If the experiences completed up to now are examined, not only in Europe but also in other areas of the world, it would be difficult to categorize them under one or two models. Similarly, as regards the prospects of other peoples' advance to socialism, it strikes me we should be careful not to set up one or more new models to be followed schematically. Even for the countries of Europe, which we have discussed so much and in which conditions are rather similar in many respects, we have not raised the issue of elaborating together—Communists and socialists—any single model. We believe that certain shared needs and directions, concerning both the mode of approaching socialism and the kind of socialism to be constructed, can and should be developed. We believe it necessary, moreover, to clearly indicate differences with respect to previous experiences elsewhere, this being necessary to clarify our own objectives. We are convinced—you may be sure—of the need to elaborate further on the problems involved in starting a new kind of social-economic development and a transformation of a society like ours in a socialist way. The debate about these problems and their ideological and political implications can and should continue—on a European level as well—and a clearer definition of our own perspective be reached. Beyond a certain point, however, one runs the risk of playing intellectual games; we certainly don't want to commit this mistake, trying to put diapers on the world.

About the problem of relations with the past, it seems to me that the observations we made earlier on the Western European countries were very much concerned with this: the need to build on the most valid trends and achievements of previous national history (and regional history as well, in the sense of the region of Europe to which we belong) in transforming the society in the direction of socialism.

**H.** *Perhaps even to realize history potentialities not realized earlier?*

**N.** Certainly. Insofar as Italy is concerned, we have some suggestive observations from Gramsci. In his report to the last party congress, Berlinguer, for example, took up Gramsci's reflection on the positive aspects of the cosmopolitanism of Italian intellectuals. He emphasized how the universalistic tendency of our culture and our people, which has been realized only in part in the past, could be fully developed through the commitment of a new national ruling class to relating—and this would indeed be necessary—the transformation of Italian society to a movement for a growing, multiform world cooperation.

The problem of coming to terms with the past, and especially with our cultural tradtitions, has in any case been the subject of long reflection by our movement. I would say that as a question of principle, it has long ago been resolved. The cultural revolution, the formation of a new culture, cannot be conceived as an indiscriminate negation of the cultural heritage; it cannot be premised on a sort of tabula rasa. The national heritage as a whole cannot simply be appropriated uncritically. The problem arises in making choices, in identifying the tendencies, the themes of one's historical past, which seem worthwhile recuperating and in defining a method, the most valid critical approach, to making such an appraisal.

The Italian Communist Party had already begun its careful exploration of the democratic and progressive traditions in Italian history and culture during the interwar period, at the time of the antifascist struggle and during the incubation of a new strategy for itself as a leading national party. The effort to reunite itself with these national roots, and particularly to come to terms with our national cultural heritage, was developed in a far broader way after the Liberation and during the fifties. The general correctness of this effort has, in my opinion, been indisputable. The specific kinds of terms and some of the particular choices we made can be debated, however, and so can the occasionally simplistic and superficial ways in which we referred to certain aspects of our political-cultural past.

There is another question that we have to ask today about the relation with the national cultural tradition: Have the terms of the problem been changing? Twenty-five years ago, the circulation of products, influences and cultural modes coming from abroad was infinitely smaller in Italy. Italian cultural life was still relatively insular; a coming to terms with national cultural traditions therefore had an exceptional significance and impact. But today, in a country like ours, the unprecedented expansion of international cultural relations, of the world market of ideas, has to be taken into account. It has now become indispensable for a Party like ours to pay close attention to ideological and cultural influences from abroad, to succeed as well in making a critical selection of what has become a particularly significant element in the cultural formation of the masses, and especially the masses of youth.

**H.**  *Certainly, the problem is enormously complex, and there is no easy solution. The tendency—in seeking to transform the society—to behave like museum curators, picking over things to be preserved should, in my view, be avoided. A conservationist stance is important, especially as regards the physical heritage, the artistic patrimony, the historical centers, cities like Venice (all of which, as we know, have been so neglected in Italy). But the problem is not only what to conserve, but also what not to conserve.*

**N.**  And then it is not simply a question of conserving, but rather of reinstating this most precious heritage of the national past within a new cycle of cultural development.

**H.**  *Precisely, I raised the question without proposing any solutions, because there are no ready answers. I am convinced, however, that the process of social transformation involves both aspects, and the relations with the past have not always been understood in a sufficiently self-conscious and critical way. But now, having spoken about the modes and problems of a transformation in a socialist direction, I want to broaden the subject of our discussion still further. We must never forget that, especially for those who have not devoted a large part of their lives struggling for socialism, a major question remains: Why be a socialist at all, why strive for a socialist transformation of the society? Is it not possible or sufficient to make improvements in bourgeois society which has, after all—at least in the advanced countries—permitted the majority of the population a far more satisfactory standard of living than before?*

**H.**  After periods of uncertainty, even confusion about the reasons for socialism, the very events of the last few years have led us back to a comprehensive reflection on the contradictions in the mode of capitalist production, the forms of social organization and the human relations particular to capitalism. When, during the golden years of "miraculous" capitalist growth in the 1950s, several Marxist and other socialist writers propounded the need for socialism as a response to certain aspects of the human condition in capitalist societies, to the more "alienating" aspects of capitalist development, I believe they called attention to an important problem and to a significant dimension of the problem of socialism. However, with regard to the development of productive forces, the rhythm and constancy of economic growth, the employment of the labor force and the elimination of pockets of backwardness in advanced capitalist societies, they took it for granted that neocapitalism was in a position to provide a solution or some sort of guarantee. Now, we find ourselves facing the fact that capitalism is once again, indeed more than ever, showing itself incapable of ensuring balanced and continuous economic growth with the fullest utilization of productive capabilities, of guaranteeing solutions to the problems of employment and the material well being of large masses, even within the countries of the West, of keeping in check the objective contradictions inherent in the mode of capitalist production. All of this, naturally, is the result in part of pressures external to the shpere of the advanced capitalist nations. At the same time, the failure of the underdeveloped nations to take off appears as a dramatic consequence of the conditions of exploitation and dependency to which they are still subjected. The necessity of socialism and—what we were talking about earlier—specifically of a self-conscious leadership of the entire process of social development in the interests of the collectivity is thus becoming evident. It is becoming part of the consciousness of great masses and of new generations. This exercise of self-conscious leadership will fully unfold itself as we move toward the control and, in the final analysis, the collective ownership of the basic means of production and along the road of increasingly cogent democratic development of the government of the people. Socialism, defined as a society of free and equal men, should not be a mere figure of old-style political oratory.

**H.** *Socialism fraternal communities, I should add . . .*

**N.** Yes, we have to appreciate what this expression means in terms of the desire really to overcome class antagonisms. We have to recognize the moral and ideal striving for liberty and equality as a fundamental element of socialism and an undeniable aspect of its superiority.

**H.** *Here again we come back to Marx. We have not talked very much about Marx because, ca va sans dire, we are Marxists, but it should be pointed out that at this very moment the contradiction between the social character of production on a world scale and the private appropriation of wealth by particular groups is becoming enormous and increasingly critical. In the past several decades, after all, unprecedented world wide social and economic changes have taken place. One might even say that for most of the world the Middle Ages ended with the 1950s. Many of Marx's predictions about the tendencies within capitalism are now beginning to come true.*

**N.** As you know, in Italy too there has been an extraordinary wave of interest in Marxism since the end of the sixties, especially among the young. This growing familiarization with Marx and with Marxism has at times had the ingenuous tone of discovery or of the acquisition of infallible truth. However, it has unquestionably reflected a growing consciousness of the contradictions and distortions in capitalist development and, further, the profundity and possible consequences of the crisis of capitalism. With the accentuation of the crisis in recent times, the return to Marx, I would say, has often been an invaluable rediscovery for all of us. Even in works of Marx published only recently for the first time we have found extraordinary anticipations of developments in capitalism which would come decades and decades afterwards.

Some people—it is true—speak today of a crisis of Marxism. To be sure, together with the renewed influence and fortune of Marxism, we can also discern a crisis in the development of Marxist thought and analysis. But what conclusions can we draw from this? Above all, the need for the parties of the working class and Marxist intellectuals of various persuasions to pursue a more open and engaged "dialogue on Marxism" (as you called it years ago), without, however, anyone pretending to be the one true bearer of an authentic interpretation of Marx and Marxism, without anybody pretending to bestow or take away the label "Marxist" I say this, of course, keeping in mind those who would want to remove Marxist as a label for our Party, probably forgetting that we have never defined ourselves in any scholastic way as a "Marxist" party (nor Marxist-Leninist), not even in our statutes. We are a political organization, inspired by Marxism, by the ideas of Marxism, but we also admit to our membership those who do not identify with Marxist ideology, and we are open to all debates about Marxism, even with those from outside the ranks of our Party. As far as our political practice is concerned, we are waiting for someone to prove what precisely, is—I am quoting one writer—"absolutely non-Marxist" about it. The essential point is that the Party as a whole and the leading group within it are increasingly coming to grips with Marxist culture and Marxist research and seeking to stimulate its original development both within and outside of our ranks.

**H.** *I agree. Much could be said about this recent flowering of Marxism, and this perhaps is not the place to say it. However, two observations seem appropriate: First, that Marxism is not a point of arrival, but rather a point of departure, not a corpus of* *sacred texts that are referred to in order to conclude discussion, but an instrument for analyzing reality. Personally, I distrust the tendency of certain Marxists to substitute metaphysical analysis for Marx's own effort to analyze the capitalist system as it existed in his time. Second, I agree completely with your point that different analyses and solutions to particularly complex problems are possible and present within Marxism. To condemn a political movement, by defining it as non-Marxist, strikes me as meaningless and dangerous. The PCI, too, I believe, is against such excommunications of other Communist parties. Here, however, we touch on the theme of internationalism: how should it be conceived and practiced today?*

**N.** This theme is very important for a Party like ours which, while profoundly rooted in a national reality, has never considered itself apart from the development of revolutionary movements, of movements for national liberation and struggles for liberty and democracy in other parts of the world. An internationalist vision and passion has, in fact, been one of the distinctive characteristics of our party. Let me just recall what the drama and epic of Vietnam—an exemplary moment in the struggle against imperialism—meant for us and for the formation of the youth who drew close to us during the sixties.

Our internationalism has been and still is an object of reproof from various quarters even from within the Italian working class and democratic movement, almost as if it were identical with an acritical solidarity with socialist countries and Communist Parties. But our conception and practice of internationalism has come to be defined in much broader and very different terms. I have already taken the opportunity to recall how at various times, when necessary, we made public our dissent with the positions of other Communist Parties, reaffirming that when questions involving shared responsibility were at stake, we felt the need not to limit ourselves simply to expressions of formal solidarity that, in fact, concealed substantial disagreements. I also referred to our assessments of previous experiences in constructing socialism as precluding summary dismissals and, at the same time, being far removed from apologetic glorifications.

I would further like to stress the degree to which the boundaries of our internationalism have been broadened. We have sought and still seek to establish relations—beyond the range of Communist parties—with liberation movements in countries of the third world, some of which are inspired by Marxism, and others not—many of which propose socialist objectives, yet take positions and paths that are completely original. We have raised the problem, and are doing so at this very moment, of intensifying relations with socialist and social-democratic parties. We are convinced, as I already emphasized, that our experiences with the struggle for democracy and socialism are not in any way assimilable to the traditional conceptions and practice of European social democracy. The Socialist-International today includes within its ranks parties like the Italian socialist party which has dissented openly from the prevailing orientation of European social democracy, especially at the time of the Cold War; parties like the French socialist party, which have undergone profound renewal; socialist and social-democratic parties within which there are progressive positions and new lines of inquiry; in short, parties that no matter how divergent from us in their ideological positions and perspectives, represent important interlocutors in the development of a collaboration among left forces in Europe.

**H.** *Turning to the narrower problem of the relations among Communist parties: the Italian Party, under Togliatti, launched the idea of polycentrism; in the last decade, however, the Communist movement has divided rather than developing in a polycentric way. I am not sure whether one can even speak of a world*

*Communist movement at this point. What is the PCI's attitude to this situation?*

**N.** We did not hesitate to talk about a crisis in our movement at the world conference of Communist parties in 1969. There is no doubt that the conflict between China and the Soviet Union is the principal factor in a division which is fraught with many heavy consequences. Then, there are divergences and differences of opinion which have not, however, resulted in ruptures.

The Communist movement has to be seen differently from the way it was in the past. The Communist International was dissolved in 1943. It no longer existed when the Communists of my generation entered the Party; we belong to another historical epoch that cannot avoid being characterized by far less stringent, broader and more flexible forms of unity. If we want unity, it has to be achieved in diversity and through continuous debate. I mean a diversity of political as well as ideological positions, corresponding partly to the diversity of experiences and objective conditions, and partly to differences arising from the directions which the theoretical and political developments and concrete struggle for socialism or the construction of socialism have taken in various countries. I, therefore, believe that we have to understand precisely, on the one hand, the dramatic implications of problems of the kind posed by the estrangement of the Chinese Communist Party from the majority of Communist parties, and on the other the need to consider the diversity of positions among Communist parties that still maintain cooperative relations as an undramatic, but inevitable fact, to be accepted as such. It is important, moreover, that these diverse positions be debated more openly, more consistently without leading to excommunications, clearing the ground of whatever misunderstandings and ambiguities there might be and holding out the possibility of further discussion of pending questions. This strikes me as the way that the needs and prospects of the world Communist movement have to be considered today.

**H.**   *Don't the disputes also involve questions of an ideological nature such as the relationship to Leninism?*

**N.**   In dealing with Leninism, one would have to talk about the polemics and debates this theme has generated not only among the range of Communist parties, but also within a broader range of forces on the left. We are faced with those who want us to swear by Leninism and those who want us to abjure it. We believe that both demands are unacceptable. It is not a question of swearing by Leninism, understood as a closed body of doctrine.

**H.**   *The term was not even invented by Lenin. The very word "Leninism" was coined by Zinoviev and then picked up by Stalin.*

**N.**   Certain absurd ways of dogmatizing Lenin's thought have to be combated. And that is what we have been attempting to do. I can recollect an extremely significant article written to this end by Togliatti in 1960, also the recent contributions we made to discussions on Lenin and Leninism on the occasion of the hundredth anniversary of his birth. Lenin himself provides weapons for the battle against turning his thought into dogma. On many occasions, he was explicit and categorical in demanding concrete and original analyses of concrete situations, in rejecting the tendency to spew forth revolutionary slogans or pore over texts in search of answers with no bearing on specific day-to-day problems. Naturally, this does not mean that we can limit ourselves to drawing solely on Lenin for indications of method. We have to come to terms with his analysis of certain aspects of contemporary historical and social reality in order to be able to single out what is still valid and what has not held up to later verification or been superseded by more recent developments. His analysis of imperialism is a case in point.

Those who polemicize against our view of Leninism in Italy and abroad frequently indulge in the worst commonplaces, the worst deformations of the work of Lenin, almost as if Lenin had been a dispenser of prescriptions for revolutionary activity, a sort of technical advisor for insurrectionary movements and not a powerful, original Marxist thinker in addition to being a great revolutionary leader who has to be referred to by anybody coming to terms with the problematic of socialist struggle. Right away our touching ground with the analysis or method of Lenin is taken as proof of our diabolical duplicity, as if all of our positions on democracy and the relationship between democracy and socialism had been repudiated. We are fully aware of the fact that our conception of the relation between democracy and socialism does not correspond with that elaborated by Lenin. But this conception has been developed, not by abandoning Lenin's method, but by taking stock of profoundly different historical conditions which Lenin himself could never have predicted.

**H.**  *But even the socialists polemicize with your Leninism, if I am not mistaken.*

**N.**  The socialist movement's polemic with the Communist movement and the PSI's with the PCI has historical roots; it goes back fifty or more years to the time of the great split and the important choices taking place with the formation of the Communist parties of the Third International. It is a fact that the choice of Leninism marked at the time a major turning point in the history and the development of the international workers' movement. Should we reflect now on the historical significance of that moment, on the value and consequences those choices had? It is always possible to do so. But today it seems to me that the problem of evaluating Lenin's work, thought and teachings has to be posed by Communists and socialists alike in far more objective terms.

At present, there are some who tend to exaggerate the value of what is polemically defined as PSI revisionism, contrasting it to the dogmatism that ostensibly kept the Communist party from questioning certain Marxist or "orthodox" Leninist tenets for so long. We Communists supposedly have done no more of late than to have arrived twenty years behind time at the same conclusions reached by the Socialist Party at the end of the 1950s. But this is a polemical simplification that doesn't hold. The journey of both of our parties has been far more complex. Our Leninist matrix and our concern to conserve the maximum rigor in formulating our positions of principle have helped keep us from skipping into politically dangerous attitudes and behavior, but they have not prevented us from undertaking courageous innovations in the development of theory, strategic positions and political action.

Have we had moments of embarassment in this effort at innovation? Certainly. Have Italian socialists made original contributions in elaborating on problems, in defining perspectives in the struggle for democracy and socialism? Certainly. Our own elaboration has always been stimulated in one way or another by the presence and positions of the Socialist Party. This reciprocal influence has been continuous and profound. To the extent to which there exists a common vision of the questions of democracy and socialism, it is difficult to differentiate sharply between the contributions of each. What matters most now is to push forward with discussions between Communists and socialists—on those aspects that still divide us or have as yet to be resolved— and, in such a way, continue the ongoing search for innovative solutions to the problems of Italian society: a search which has to be conducted together with other forces of democratic persuasion, be they Catholic or lay. We Communists are not motivated by the presumption that, on our own, we alone have provided or can provide the answers to such problems, today or in the future.

# V

**HOBSBAWM:** *Let me give you an opportunity to bring your views about the status of the Italian Communist Party up to date, since our original interview took place some time ago.*

*My first question concerns the elections of 1976: What, in your opinion, are the significance and achievements of these elections?*

**NAPOLITANO:** Everybody in Italy as well as abroad has grasped the exceptional importance of our Party's success in the elections of 1976. No Communist Party in a capitalist nation in Western Europe had ever succeeded in gaining more than a third of the vote. In Italy over the past decades there had been a constant advance by the Party, but gains had previously been limited or relatively modest. From 1953 through the 1960s, the Italian electorate shifted slowly. This time, however, there was a massive shift, which had been signalled a year earlier in 1975 in the results of the regional and municipal elections.

One might have expected that the Communist Party would have had considerable difficulty in achieving similar results in national elections. One might have thought that at least part of the electorate that voted Communist in the regional and administrative elections of 1975 would have hesitated to repeat that vote for the PCI in the parliamentary elections. The stakes were higher in voting for parliament, and the vote was far more decisive. In 1976 we not only confirmed the success of 1975, but we even improved on it. Moreover, the endorsement was widespread in the traditionally left-oriented regions and other regions of the North as well as in the whole of the South. The country clearly demonstrated an electoral trend toward political unification and a leftward movement.

Still, these were not the only results of the 1976 elections. If we overlook other aspects of the outcome, we cannot understand later developments in the political situation. The elections reconfirmed the Christian Democratic Party (DC) as the party of the relative majority, although the gap between the DC and the PCI greatly diminished.

How did the DC succeed in recuperating the losses of the previous year in the regional and administrative elections? To summarize briefly, the DC succeeded in exploiting anti-Communist sentiments and the distrust and fear of a part of the electorate and the middle classes; at the same time, it succeeded in arousing in the most progressive part of its own electorate hope and faith in the possible renewal of the Christian Democratic Party itself and a potential change in its national policy. Many voters believed the DC would be more willing in 1976 to favor those reforms which it had not favored and had, in fact, boycotted in the past.

We now find ourselves faced with a rather complex situation: on the one hand, our success is a salient characteristic of the elections; on the other hand, there is a very difficult political equilibrium with the DC. It has shifted to somewhat more progressive positions under the new party secretary and partially modified the party line, but nonetheless during the electoral campaign the DC committed itself not to form a government with the Communists.

We have a rather inflexible and delicate situation. Some people during the electoral campaign envisaged a left-wing government, notwithstanding the fact that we Communists stated that we thought it neither advisable nor possible to establish a government of the left with a majority of 51 percent of the vote. In any case, the electoral results cut short the argument, because the Communists and socialists—despite the great leap ahead—did not achieve 50 percent of the vote. Even a DC-PSI majority proved impossible, so there could be no new version of the earlier center-left government with a more leftist position. The efforts to reconstitute the old four-party coalition of the center-left failed due to the opposition not only of the socialists but also of republicans. Finally, our proposal—also advanced by socialists—for a government of national emergency, composed of all antifascist parties, was rejected by the Christian Democrats. This led to a dead end from which the only solution was a one-party minority Christian Democratic government which could survive a vote of confidence or any other parliamentary crisis only through the abstention of the other antifascist parties.

The Christian Democratic Party appears in a new role: It is the ruling party, but it can govern only through the abstention of Communists and other parties.

For the first time in parliament, we heard the following: A President of the Council, who at the moment of the vote of confidence instead of using the ritual formula, "I ask for a vote of confidence from the parliament," stood up and said, "I ask for a vote of confidence and a vote of no-nonconfidence." As we know, most of the "opposition," including the Communists, abstained.

Before the new government was constituted, several important innovations were established. We insisted that the old prejudices against Communists in parliament be abandoned as a condition for resolving the governmental crisis. This was our first important political success following the elections of June 20. The Communists publicly entered the leadership of parliament. For the first time in many decades in Europe a Communist leader, Pietro Ingrao, was elected president of a chamber of parliament and several other Communists were elected to chair parliamentary committees. This was not simply a matter of prestige; it had practical importance as well.

After June 20, we wanted to stress how necessary it was that parliament once again become the fundamental center of decision making, that it acquire more power of initiative and control in opposition to the government. We achieved this and the increase in our deputies and senators together with the assumption of new responsibilities in the leadership of parliamentary activity, allowing us to exercise a decisive function. All this made the idea of a one-party Christian Democratic government retaining power—thanks to our absention—more intolerable.

In fact, in the months since, we have been able to exercise far greater initiative and control over the government than in the past. This has represented, let us say, a partial compensation for such an anomalous solution to the governmental crisis. Through parliament, not only as a Communist Party but also in agreement with other democratic forces, we have been able to indicate to the government what choices to make and what decisions to take, even often to correct the decisions of the government that seemed to us unsatisfactory. There is not doubt that since June 20 the situation in parliament has been far more open. There are greater possibilities of contesting governmental decisions and greater possibilities of agreement among the various parties, between the abstaining parties and the DC. There has been established a more systematic method of prior consultation between the government and the parties which in various ways support it. We should not exaggerate the value of this kind of agreement. As time goes on, it develops serious limitations.

**H.** *How far do you think that the present situation represents an approach to the "historic compromise" that the party favored,* *and in what relation does the present formula stand to this "historic compromise"?*

**N.** In the first place, I should like to recall that in the course of the 1976 electoral campaign, we took what I believe was a rather important position, even speaking electorally. We said that by "historical compromise" we meant a long-term collaboration of the principal components of the democratic and popular movements of our country to guarantee the unity of the broadest masses of the Italian people—the unity of the Communist, socialist and Catholic masses, as well as unity with other representative cultural and political currents whose purpose was the gradual but profound transformation of Italian society. In any case, the immediate objective that we proposed and for which we campaigned was a government of democratic solidarity that could in the short and medium range, for a few years at least, confront the nation's crisis and succeed in elaborating and implementing satisfactory solutions to the very grave problems which this crisis has brought to the surface and accentuated. At the conclusion of this experience, all of the parties would be better able to define their positions and all would be free to choose their own paths. Furthermore, perhaps this experience of several years of government in common during such a profound crisis might also clear many obstacles and open the way—if all agreed —to a more clear and certain choice directed towards what we have called the "historic compromise." That is what we said during the electoral campaign: we defined the prospect and limited the objectives. I think that this was useful, because even people who for various reasons had reservations about the "historical compromise" as a long-term solution realized the need for a reunification of democratic forces, at least for this acute phase of the crisis.

Nonetheless, following June 20, we did not achieve even the government of democratic solidarity. Instead, we have this most singular and "anomalous" situation of a government by abstention. This does not mean, however, that relations among the parties, and especially between the PCI and the DC, between the one-party Demochristian government and the Communist Party, have not changed as a result. There have been changes. For the first time, we have begun to discuss seriously the problems of governing. That, in my opinion, fits within the logic and the perspective of the "historic compromise" (I use this phrase because we coined it, and it has become popular even outside of Italy).

Within the DC today there is much division and uncertainty. I am not making a distinction of the old type between left currents and right currents in that party, partly because today it is very difficult to say which positions within the DC are authentically left and which are substantially on the right. One should rather speak of realistic currents which have recently assumed greater prominence with the DC. New groups and new men in that party have demonstrated their ability to take stock rather coldly of the new political realities in Italy, such as the growth in the seriousness and ability to govern demonstrated by the PCI. I would say that these realists are the forces which support the experiment of the Andreotti government more or less loyally (because within the DC so many other factors, such as rivalries and personal and group counterpositions, are at work). The Andreotti government is politically supported by those Christian democratic forces who believe it necessary to take account of the greater strength and the greater assumption of responsibility by the PCI.

**H.** *It seems to me that the PCI is in a rather ambiguous position now, being in some sense involved in government and in some sense not involved in government. What are the main problems that have arisen for the PCI out of this anomalous position which you yourself described?*

**N.** The first problem, now very obvious, is that we can only influence government policy very partially and negatively. Our capacity to influence future government decisions is limited. We are not in a position to contribute to the construction of a more organic, programmatic and political line of the government, and we are not in a position to participate actively in carrying out the commitments undertaken by the government. The result is obviously embarrassing: We are co-responsible for the birth and survival of this government, yet we cannot guarantee that this government will formulate the needed programs or carry them out with continuity and coherence or take the necessary decisions as the occasion arises. Clearly, the whole problem is aggravated by the economic, social and moral crisis that the country has been undergoing for several years. If the situation were more normal, the fact that we are not in the government, that there is no real majority, that there is an unsatisfactory governmental program (though at least one partly responding to our demands), and so on, would be less serious. Instead, the complexity and profundity of the crisis in Italy today demands very delicate and certainly unpopular decisions as well as an effort at more long-range planning. It is precisely at this level that the difficulties and deficiencies of the government are most obvious. Here also there are the greatest possibilities of contradiction for us. Unpopular decisions must be made, because in Italy there is a high rate of inflation, a structural deficit in the balance of payments that becomes worse as production picks up and because public finances are in a chaotic state, which reflects the growth of parasitism and subsidies which have produced grave distortions of the general development of the country.

We have tried to find solutions to these problems. We have tried to indicate ways out of the crisis in its most acute forms. It must be admitted that fundamentally our answers have converged with those of other parties, at least with their public statements: the need to transfer resources from consumption to productive investments, the need in particular to reduce nonessential individual consumption, the need to make hard choices in public expenditures, to reorganize the administration of the revenue and fiscal systems and, more generally, the need to reform the public administration and the structures of the state.

On these fundamental points, the parties are in theoretical agreement, but the question is how in practice resources are to be actually transferred from individual consumption to investment (for instance, should it be through extraordinary fiscal measures?) and how to introduce criteria of social equity in the definition of these measures.

In the past months, we have pressed these points with partial success. Beyond that, what the workers who follow us certainly demand is a stronger guarantee that things will move in the directions we have indicated and on which other parties have shown agreement. Emergency measures are not enough, even if we assume that those emergency measures are in themselves sufficiently equitable. From this point of view, among others, the working masses would feel they had a better guarantee if we were in the government together with other parties, in a position to exert pressure and directly contribute to the coherent development of a policy of recovery and renewal.

**H.** *But is there not a tendency for some people to say, "Why should the CP, which is not in the government, take the responsibility for some of these unpopular measures? Why should it not remain in opposition? Why should it risk losing popularity among many people who have voted for it and many people who might vote for it but are not satisfied with the present situation?"*

**N.** There have been a lot of discussions on this point, particularly last October and November. I took part in many of them. You will recall that in September, 1976, there was a sudden drop in the value of the *lira* on the market, a sudden aggravation of the country's financial situation. That is when the government took those emergency fiscal measures to which I have just referred. We discussed them with many thousands of workers and others of our voters in a great many meetings. I think that this was a high point in our party life and in our relationship with the masses. They were not easy discussions, but in the end we achieved substantial clarification of those very points which you raised in your question. How did we reply to the objections? We replied by thoroughly analyzing the economic-financial and economic-social crisis of the country. We explained its seriousness and emphasized the necessity of immediate intervention in that crisis. We said that we must on no account underestimate the consequences that a further aggravation of the crisis would have for the labor movement, the working masses and for the cause of democracy. If inflation went above the rate of 20 percent, if we approached the rates of inflation typical of certain Latin American countries, then there would be no way of telling how far the deterioration even of the political situation in Italy would go. Furthermore, we said, if the deficit in our balance of payments worsened, if our foreign accounts worsened, then we would be forced to rely even more heavily on foreign loans—but under what conditions and with what consequences for the national independence of our country?

I believe that to the degree that the working class—the workers who follow us—became aware of the depth of the crisis and the necessity of not letting it fester and come to a head, there also developed a greater understanding of our attitude. In fact, the second point on which we insisted was this: Can we as Communists stand aside in such a situation merely because we are not wanted in the government? After the elections of June 20, the argument that we should remain in opposition could not be put to the test. If we had chosen opposition, there would have been no majority and no government. There would only have been new elections immediately and those in a more dangerous political and an ever more serious economic, financial and social situation.

We persisted in these arguments, and in the last months of 1976 we obtained growing support among our active membership and our voters. What we had chosen to do was not to line up behind the politics of the government but to offer instead critical confrontation with the government from an autonomous position. In so doing, the Party took full responsibility for the need to do something immediately—today and not tomorrow— to intervene in the crisis. Its further aggravation must be prevented. Steps to prepare its gradual overcoming must be taken.

**H.** *But, in fact, have there not arisen particular difficulties— say, in the trade unions or in your relations with students and other groups—in recent months?*

**N.** Yes, there have been many instances of difficulties and discussions within the trade unions, in the relations between trade unions and workers, and also in the relations between trade unions and various parties, including our own. On the other hand, it is very important to note that in all these months we were successful in realizing an effective defense of the interests and rights of the working class. Let it be recalled that even in 1975—a year of grave recession with a fall in industrial production and national income unequalled since the early postwar years—even in 1975, notwithstanding the considerable drop in productivity together with that of industrial production, we had an increase in real wages. Not only did we protect wages from inflation but we also succeeded in increasing them in real terms. Despite the fall of productive activity in 1975, we largely succeeded in defending the levels of employment. All this was made possible thanks to two fundamental conditions: on the one hand, an escalator clause an automatic adjustment of wages to the cost-of-living index which precisely in 1975 was further improved, and on the other hand, the system of unemployment insurance and strong union bargaining power, which prevented mass dismissals and guaranteed even to workers who were not needed a wage very close to the normal. In 1976 we had a further increase in real wages, despite a level of inflation above 16 percent. It is true that some price increases have not been fully offset through the escalator clause (for example, the cost of gasoline is not included in the index). It is also true that we have agreed to freeze completely wage increases based on the cost of living for those with annual salaries above 8 million *lire* about $9,300 at the current official exchange rate; actually somewhat higher in terms of real purchasing power and 50 percent of that increase for those with annual salaries above 6 million *lire* about $7,000 at the current exchange rate. However, this means that for the majority of workers whose earnings are below these levels we have succeeded in avoiding substantial sacrifices and, indeed, have obtained further improvements for them.

The most serious problems arise rather with regard to other social strata: on the one hand, with the middle classes who have been quite justly asked to make some sacrifices and, on the other hand, with the unemployed and the "marginalized", especially youth and students seeking work, those with high-school diplomas or college degrees. The South and the Southern Question are a crucially important aspect of this. As you know, they are central to the problem of unemployment and also to the new processes of the growth of social marginality.

Finally, there is the problem of the possible divisions within the mass of the employed workers themselves. I already discussed some of these questions with you, Eric, in our first interview in the fall of 1975. We are in a period in which the consolidation and development of the politics of alliance of the working class is not easy. Here I recall Gramsci's passage on the working class, which in order to cement its hegemony must take account of the interests of the social strata with which it intends to establish a hegemonic alliance. To do this, workers must be prepared to make sacrifices of an economic-corporative nature, but on the other hand they must not renounce their essential role, which is to assert leadership in the places of production and in the other centers of fundamental decisions.

This is a point which we have recently dealt with in practice. When it was realized that extraordinary fiscal measures were necessary, we could have argued that the working class should pay nothing or, on the contrary, that only the working class should be called upon to make sacrifices in order to maintain its alliances, especially with the middle groups. In fact, however, the problem was and is to establish an equilibrium whereby neither objective nor subjective conditions would exist which would require the working class to make sacrifices without the middle sectors also paying a price for the crisis: At the same time, we had to combat tendencies which do exist at present in the working class to unload the weight of the crisis solely on the middle sectors on the grounds that the middle sectors have up to now enjoyed far better conditions than the working class. We have been and still are engaged in the search for a point of equilibrium between the defense of the interests of the working class, a correct division of concessions between the working class and the middle sectors (and other social strata) and the consolidation of the politics of alliance of the working class and the whole alignment of democratic forces.

We have also had to face sectarian pressures within the working class as well as corporative ("economistic") tendencies. What I mean is the tendency to see one's own problems in a narrow and sectional manner. We are troubled about this. Remember that within the Italian context a number of unjustified inequities between different categories of workers have been accumulating. These must be resolved in the interests of the unity of the workers' movement and in view of the crisis facing the country. Still, the trade unions in order to lessen certain indefensible sectional privileges for some workers have made courageous decisions. I will give you a single example. Recently the decision was made to abolish the special escalator clause mechanisms enjoyed by some workers (such as bank employees, railroad and trolley workers and selected workers in the chemical industry). These were mechanisms, special agreements, by which these job categories had a more advantageous escalator clause than all other industrial workers enjoyed.

I should mention those corporative tendencies which lead people to see their own problems as employed workers outside of the general economic and social context, i.e. to forget how important a part of this context is the phenomenon of unemployment, especially unemployment in the South, the unemployment of women and of young people. We have always said, and recently this has been reiterated by top union leaders, that the trade union cannot be thought of as an organization merely for the defense of employed workers—this is a very important point—but it must also be considered as an organization for the defense of unemployed workers and young people looking for work. Unfortunately, the efforts to make this point of view prevail have been realized only in part. It is true that while the trade unions have agreed on the need to contain wage increases they have strongly insisted that the demands of the employed workers must be pressed on another level, that is, regarding controls over investment and the development of a new economic policy capable of guaranteeing an increase in employment. It is also true that in 1976, when the major industrial labor contracts were renewed, new rights for the trade unions were won regarding investment programs within the enterprises, and the unions pledged themselves to exercise these rights above all toward the end of increasing productive investments in the South and increasing the level of employment.

Still, we must say that the very application of these contracts, the actual establishment of these rights and the practical development of this approach—a struggle for investment and employment—are not simple. They are very difficult in themselves because the policies of the government do not offer a valid frame of reference. Furthermore, there is the resistance of the companies, beginning with the larger industrial enterprises. They avoid discussions of these programs with labor representatives, or they avoid serious commitments to make investments in the South or to increase employment. Beyond all these objective difficulties, whether political or entrepreneurial, it must still be said that the working class has not been entirely convinced of the importance of these objectives and of this battle. This conviction is essential in order to avoid a separation and rupture between employed workers and the unemployed, especially in the South and among the youth and students.

**H.** *In the meantime the Communist Party has become much more influential in the government of various regions and big cities than before. Could you perhaps tell us a little of what has been happening in these regions since we last spoke?*

**N.** There are unquestionably a number of new and important developments in the regions and communes which the Communists have been called upon to govern for the first time, along with other parties, primarily the Socialist Party. There have been important and positive advances toward a new style of running local and regional government, aimed at arousing greater democratic participation and more acceptable methods of administration. There has been a dedicated effort to resolve the heavy indebtedness of many local governing bodies. The biggest problem in the regions has been and still is how to obtain more powers and finances from the central government and the right to use those powers and finances more effectively.

A very large question arises when one considers the administrations of the large cities from Turin to Naples, which we found in disastrous condition. I think of the difficulties which we have encountered in administering these cities, and then I think of the difficulties which we face in confronting the great national problems in parliament and in our relationship with the government. In some of the discussions which I have had in recent months in Turin, Genoa, Milan, Pisa, Naples, at a certain point I myself have asked this question: "Couldn't we avoid burdening ourselves with all this dead weight from the past?" My answer to it is this: If we can detach ourselves for a moment from the situation—a very difficult, dark and uncertain situation full of risks and politically very tense—we can say that an historical process however tortuous and meandering is underway involving the gradual replacement of the ruling class of our country. New social and political forces—basically the working class and the principal party of the working class—are assuming the roles of leadership, are becoming part of a new ruling class under conditions of difficult equilibrium and even of necessary compromise with other and older social and political forces. If this is indeed the case, then we must answer that never in history have new ruling classes assumed leadership of a society without the existence of a deep crisis in the old ruling classes, without the collapse or corrosion of old regimes. There has never been a case of the accession of new social and political forces to leadership of society, whether in classical revolutionary forms or in peaceful forms, when things were going in the best of all possible ways. This has never happened.

Today we are indeed facing a very difficult legacy; but in history there are no legacies which new classes and social forces on the rise can refuse. They can only be accepted courageously as part of the prospect of the transformation of society.

**H.** *Let me ask you my last question. Since we last spoke there has been a great deal of talk about Eurocommunism, especially since the summit meeting, if I may call it that, in Madrid be-*

*tween the Spanish, French and Italian Communist Parties. At the same time, there have been a number of international problems within the Communist movement, particularly in relation to human rights in East Europe and so on. How far have these changed, modified or caused further development in the attitudes of the Italian Communist Party?*

**N.** I would say both developments are related to what I said in our first interview on the PCI. It seems to me that we spoke rather at length on the need to identify certain fundamental points of common commitment of the Communist Parties of Western Europe and a common characterization of the strategy of these parties. We have made progress in this direction. Naturally we can discuss the definition of Eurocommunism; the word can mean many things. I think that the best definition of Eurocommunism is as an original and coherent effort of the Communist Parties of Western Europe, the Communist Parties in this part of the world, to seek out and travel a road to socialism which will guarantee the full development of the best and highest political and cultural traditions and the most advanced social and democratic conquests of Western Europe.

I would like to add something to this. Recently, we have had indications of growing interest in our ideas from some non-European Communist Parties, for example the Japanese Communist Party. We have succeeded in composing a joint declaration of our two Parties, which contains many of the fundamental points of the declarations which we wrote in common with the Spanish and French Parties. To me, that means that even outside of Europe there are common problems in the advanced capitalist countries and that, therefore, even in a Party like the Japanese one can identify with certain aspects of a strategy similar to the one developed by Communist Parties in the advanced capitalist countries of Western Europe.

With regard to your other question, we have sought to carry

forward seriously and responsibly, without fanfare, our line of support for democratic principles and of support of the need for a new and further development of democratic practice in the socialist countries. We do not believe that we are obliged to accept the thesis that expression of our opinion on serious cases of the grave violation of individual rights and democratic liberties in a socialist country represents an unacceptable interference in its affairs. When these values and principles are at stake, we hold that it is our duty clearly to express our opinion and dissent. Actually, we believe that it is in the vital interests of the socialist countries to solve these problems correctly. We hold that failure to resolve problems of this nature constitutes a source of grave internal and international weakness.

**H.**  *Is there anything else you would like to say to round off this supplement to your views on the PCI?*

**N.**  I should like to say only this: We are very much aware not of a sense of precariousness (because we believe that our political action has built important solid things in Italy) but of a sense of difficulty and risk. We know that even solid constructions and conquests can be endangered. We also know that there can be sudden reversals of tendency in the Italian situation. Of course, there can also be regression on the level of international relations; there may also be steps backward with regard to the development of international détente, and this would obviously have serious effects in every country, especially in Italy. Even apart from this last aspect, the economic, social and political fragility of our country is real—and so are its contradictions. The political and class struggle here is always extremely acute, even if it sometimes appears to be hidden. Then too, certain powerful, ruthless and unscrupulous forces external to Italy follow developments here and seek to influence them. Thus, we must be vigilant; we must never give in to conceit or any form of excessive self-confidence—or worse yet to bureaucratic complacency.

We cannot afford illusions. Everything we have achieved and won has cost so much energy and hard work. We must continue in this struggle day by day to move forward and not be pushed back, so that we can develop our democracy and not see it crushed to death.